LET'S GET TO KNOW HIM

A JOURNEY TO KNOWING GOD

Sharon Loyd and
Sheri Edwards

WESTBOW
PRESS®
A DIVISION OF THOMAS NELSON
& ZONDERVAN

Scripture taken from the King James Version of the Bible.

WestBow Press books may be ordered through booksellers or by contacting:

WestBow Press
A Division of Thomas Nelson & Zondervan
1663 Liberty Drive
Bloomington, IN 47403
www.westbowpress.com
1 (866) 928-1240

ISBN: 978-1-5127-9520-2 (sc)
ISBN: 978-1-5127-9519-6 (hc)
ISBN: 978-1-5127-9521-9 (e)

Library of Congress Control Number: 2017910691

Print information available on the last page.

WestBow Press rev. date: 8/9/2017

CONTENTS

ACKNOWLEDGEMENTS

The summer of 1959 was a life changing summer for me as I turned 13 and received Christ as my *personal* Savior. My Dad suffered a broken back from a freak accident that same summer and had to move our family from Clay County, Florida to Marion County. I was heartbroken to leave my church and friends but because of my new life in Christ, I began to read my Bible through and while reading the Bible through, my eyes were opened to the world of writing! That next summer, I met Terry Loyd. I will always be thankful for his encouragement to me to keep writing even through the darkest days of my life. We were married in 1964. Terry is my Sunday school teacher, my confidant and advisor. We are a team. God blessed us with two daughters, Sheri Edwards and Stephanie Cumbie. My daughters and husband are all writers. Sheri and Mark, her husband, are missionaries to Lages, Brazil. Sheri challenged me to write a daily blog with her for one full year. And so, our journey "Let's Get to Know Him" began as we searched the scriptures, daily, for others to know, really know, this God of ours! Stephanie and her husband, Greg Cumbie, are my cheerleaders. Stephanie's understanding of grammar and sentence structure is amazing. I thank the Lord Jesus Christ, FIRST, but need to also acknowledge these family members, especially my husband. I admit that I could not and cannot do what I do without him! Lastly, I thank Lillian Sivley for always, always encouraging me to write and finish my first novel, "Somebody, Please." What true friends she and her husband, John, have been to our family!

Sharon Loyd

To Mark, Mrs. Delores and Brazil: The three of you are why I know God better today and why I want to know Him better tomorrow. May the prospect of souls motivate us towards that moment when God's eyes rest upon our faces and He says, "Well done."

Sheri Edwards

PREFACE

"Let's Get to Know Him"
By Sharon Loyd and Sheri Edwards

Sharon Loyd and Sheri Edwards have collaborated together to create a powerful presentation of one's personal relationship with God. Often, when a mother-daughter collaborate on a book, it is very one sided in the dominance of one personality, while the other seems to be only a support in this volume, they both have powerfully written from their perspective positions in life. As there is no contradiction with God and HIS Word, there is no contradiction in the writing of these two influential authors. Instead, they show biblically by example and well thought out principle, based on the Word of God, how one can have their own personal relationship with God.

First and foremost, they present these thoughts on the foundation that one's relationship with God is very personal. God is a Spirit. We are created in His image. We can get to know HIM so well, that HIS voice in our heart is as familiar to our heart as our spouse's and children's voices are to our ears.

Starting out with *Every Road Needs a Map*, they rightly point out that life's road cannot be traversed successfully unless we follow the LORD's will and way. Where God leads us in life will never contradict His Word. The relationship can become so strong, that when there are **bumps in the road**, the LORD is there. HE gives peace and strength. These ladies give examples of how God led them through their trials. Their examples and Biblical instruction help prepare the reader find that the same Biblical principles will sustain them in the crucible of life's trials.

Each chapter focuses on the journey. The book is not about the moment; rather it is about having eternity set in your heart. The toughness of the journey of life is like a marriage of years. The strength of body and beauty of skin in youth will be replaced with life that is stronger than death, and beauty of spirit that is a foundation for others to build upon, showing that the will of God according to HIS Word is always right. As the relationships of life with your spouse and others grow, your relationship with God will grow so intimate, that the day of one's death is merely the day of entering the presence of the glory of God for eternity, awaiting others you love to follow.

Dr. Andy Bloom-Pastor of Central Baptist Church, Ocala, Florida

PACK YOUR BAGS!

Your bag is packed with your favorite Bible and journal, and our journey begins. In order to receive all that the Lord has for us, we must begin in His dwelling place! Is it a new year for you, or are you in a summer slump? It doesn't matter, because our God is there right beside you and me. He longs for you to know Him, really know Him. "He that dwelleth in the secret place of the most High shall abide under the shadow of the Almighty. I will say of the Lord, He is my refuge and my fortress: my God; in him will I trust" (Psalm 91:1–2)

First Kings 8:49 reaffirms God's dwelling place as Heaven, "Then hear thou their prayer and their supplication in heaven thy dwelling place, and maintain their cause."

We can't travel up to heaven (yet), but God is with us through Jesus Christ, His Son, our Savior. The Holy Spirit of the living God resides in those who have received Him as Savior. So, how is your soul doing? I'm sure after cleaning your house, mowing the grass, changing the diapers—no wait, we just throw them away—and checking the pantry with menu in hand, you are worn down, and it doesn't seem you are anywhere *near* the Lord or care where He dwells. You just want to put your feet up before you have to load the washer again. Am I right? Our bodies definitely require a comfortable dwelling place as well. Wouldn't you agree?

But you know what? Our souls need a calm dwelling place even more than our bodies do. This inward comfort, as you well know, is of far greater importance than the outward. The inward, your soul and my soul, can be full of peace, joy, and rest. God tells us so. And if we want to get to know Him better, we are going to have to realize that it requires something from us. There isn't a magic dust we can sprinkle! I know, what a real downer! That would be so easy!

Now, imagine we are pulling up to your favorite coffee shop. While you take a quick break, read more about this "dwelling place of God" in 2 Chronicles 6: 2, 21, 30–42. Get your journal out. Do you see Him in these words? Do you hear Him? Write it down before you forget.

This part of our trip will require two things:

1. We must *dwell* in Him if we want to claim the promises He gives when we do surrender to Him this year!

2. We must *commit* to Him. Release yourself from the worry of what surrounds you. This will be impossible if you do not *trust* in his dwelling place.

These are two simple thoughts to take with you on this first day of your journey: dwell and commit.

Dwell on God and in God by reading and obeying the truth that is in His Word. He has the welcome mat out and the door open. He is inviting you to get to know Him.

"Come unto me, all ye that labour and are heavy laden, and I will give you rest. Take my yoke upon you, and learn of me; for I am meek and lowly in heart: and ye shall find rest unto your souls. For my yoke is easy and my burden is light" (Matthew 11:28–30).

Commit to the fact that God wants you to know Him. He wants to be that safe dwelling place for you, no matter what kind of baggage you are bringing with you. But you have to be willing to commit to what He tells you to do. Are you?

Keep your bags packed as we travel together and enter into God's dwelling place. The load will become lighter, I promise! Just remember: dwell and commit. You aren't alone on this trip.

Next, we are going to look at the map and find out just where we are! Don't skip the scriptures! Read each one and hear this amazing God of yours.

Until next time, Lord willing,

Sharon

IS YOUR MAP UPSIDE DOWN?

Have you heard the saying "new year, new you"? Usually about this time of the year, the TV commercials and magazines begin targeting women and their weight. Marketing ploys home in on those holiday pounds we just put on, and they prey on our vulnerabilities about the upcoming bathing-suit season. One fine January morning while you happily remove your Christmas decorations, you hear that phrase on the television in the background: "It's a new year. Why not a new you?" Your lighthearted mood is promptly replaced with a slight frown as you remove the wreath from the front door. Suddenly, guilty images of yourself flash through your mind and begin to horrify you— all that midnight tiptoeing into the kitchen for a snatch of that delicious turkey or running your finger through the cheesecake when no one was looking! As you cringe in despair, your eyes land on that treadmill you got for Christmas last year, and you begin making excuses for why it is covered in laundry, craft boxes, and mail. By the time you finish shoving the boxes and tree into the attic, you catch a glimpse of yourself in the mirror—and the next thing you know, you are digging in your purse for your cell phone and dialing up your BFF to see if she wants to join Weight Watchers with you. All because of some phrase that made you start thinking about a "new you."

So, my fellow weight-crazed female friend, let's take a reality check. Before we head out on this trip, we need to look at the map and find out where we are and where we are going. I know. I know. We really could use a new haircut and a new dress size. Truth be told, I have a box of L'Oréal #10 on my dresser, and my arm flab wiggles when I wave, but let's not worry about those problems this morning. It *is* a new year for you, but not everything has to change about us! Let's make sure our map isn't upside down so that we have a correct perspective of where we really are.

"And this is the confidence that we have in him, that, if we ask any thing according to his will, he heareth us: And if we know that he hear us, whatsoever we ask, we know that we have the petitions that we desired of him" (1 John 5:14–15).

TRUTH #1

"And *ye are Christ's*; and *Christ is God's*" (1 Corinthians 3:23, emphasis added).

Did you read that? You belong to Christ! Christ belongs to God. These are facts that will not change like the color of our hair or the number on our bathroom scales. We are safe. We are sound. We are Christ's possession. I don't know about you, but that truth is very important to me. I will be very honest with you—sometimes I feel as though I am all alone in this world. I feel that I am weird, ugly, and a general misfit of society, both in the world and in the church. I sometimes feel that I don't belong anywhere. Even in a crowd of people who I know to be true friends, part of me feels lonely, because as a foreign missionary, I know I will not be there for long—and if I were, they might not really like me at all. I know it is very self-centered to think this way, but I want you to realize that 1 Corinthians 3:23 is what helps me when I feel that loneliness. I have a choice to give in to my "self" or believe what I know to be true. And the truth is that I belong 100 percent—lock, stock, and barrel—to *someone* who cannot abandon me and who loves me no matter what. And, if you are a Christian, then you belong to Him too. So, remind yourself about it!

TRUTH #2

"For we are his workmanship, created in Christ Jesus unto good works, which God hath before ordained that we should walk in them" (Ephesians 2:10).

When my oldest daughter was a baby, my husband decided to build her a toy box. He would come home tired from driving a lumber truck around Chicago all day, but he would go out to the garage and work on that toy box for Katie. I remember we didn't have two plug nickels to rub together, but we saved what we could to buy a three-dollar ceramic handle for the box. Mark was so proud of it when he finished. I drew and painted a toy scene on the front, and then we loaded it with Katie's toys and stuffed animals. Almost twenty years later, that box is still as sturdy as it was the day Mark put it in our daughter's room. It has held toys, books, dollhouses, firewood, and even the occasional child playing hide-and-go-seek! The color from the toy scene on the lid has faded, the ceramic is missing from the handle, and there are marks on it from all the children in some fashion, but that box is a reminder to me of Mark's sacrifice made out of love for Katie.

You and I were crafted by the hands of someone who sacrificed everything for us. We were created in love and for a purpose that God has set for our lives. We are not just wandering around on this old earth! God has something for us each to do, and His Word is our personal GPS to help us find our way. How can I be sure of that? I remind myself of the truth in Ephesians 2:10. And then I remind myself of another truth: I am not just a work of His hands, but a work is still being performed in me.

TRUTH #3

"Being confident of this very thing, that he which hath begun a good work in you will perform it until the day of Jesus Christ" (Philippians 1:6).

So I belong to Him, I am made by Him, and He is making something *of* and *in* me. But just like in 1 Samuel chapter 1 when Hannah's adversary made her fret of things that seemed to be going wrong, our adversary, the devil, wants us to fret about our imperfections. He wants to move our line of vision from God and His Word, and he wants us to begin to fret about what someone posted on Facebook or the way our husbands answered us. Or the devil wants us to dwell on how lonely we are. And the sad thing is that we let him do it every single day. So here is my last thought: Why not decide together as a team of sisters to purposefully focus on God's Word and truth? Encourage each other to *not* worry and fret. Support each other with truth. Scripture is alive, and it has a power to calm us as all the clichés in this world fall flat on our troubled souls. We need to dwell and commit to the truth, together. That is our true, undistorted map for living this year. If our map is right-side up, we will be headed in the right direction.

Here is a quick checklist:

> ✒ Let's check our car and put gas in—not diesel (I did that to my dad's car once). Let's fill up with truth and not lies. Read the Word!

"For the word of God is quick, and powerful, and sharper than any two-edged sword, piercing even to the dividing asunder of soul and spirit, and of the joints and marrow, and is a discerner of the thoughts and intents of the heart" (Hebrews 4:12).

🖋 Let's check the tire pressure. Are the bills of Christmas, college, and cell phones putting you under pressure? Lay it all out in front of God and ask Him to help you see where you can be a better steward and spend more wisely. Ask Him to give you wisdom to not end up in any more financial pitfalls. Let Him keep you on the right road of wisdom.

"I wisdom dwell with prudence, and find out knowledge of witty inventions. The fear of the LORD is to hate evil: pride, and arrogancy, and the evil way, and the froward mouth, do I hate. Counsel is mine, and sound wisdom: I am understanding; I have strength. By me kings reign, and princes decree justice. By me princes rule, and nobles, even all the judges of the earth. I love them that love me; and those that seek me early shall find me. Riches and honour are with me; yea, durable riches and righteousness" (Proverbs 8:12–18).

🖋 Let's check the mileage. Are you feeling traveled and worn? Let Him renew you with His Spirit, not what some television program or ad says.

"Bless the LORD, O my soul, and forget not all his benefits: Who forgiveth all thine iniquities;

SHARON LOYD *and* SHERI EDWARDS

who healeth all thy diseases; Who redeemeth thy life from destruction; who crowneth thee with lovingkindness and tender mercies; Who satisfieth thy mouth with good things; so that thy youth is renewed like the eagle's" (Psalm 103:2–5).

"For which cause we faint not; but though our outward man perish, yet the inward man is renewed day by day. For our light affliction, which is but for a moment, worketh for us a far more exceeding and eternal weight of glory; While we look not at the things which are seen, but at the things which are not seen: for the things which are seen are temporal; but the things which are not seen are eternal" (2 Corinthians 4:16–18).

Let's remember *where* we are, *who* we are in His eyes, and *what* He wants to perfect in our lives. If you need to throw out some old thinking or just remind yourself of forgotten truths, I urge you to join me as I do the same. I promise we won't get lost, and the end will be worth the trip.

More nuggets to read: Galatians 1:1–9 and Titus 2:11–14.

Until next time, Lord willing,

Sheri

PACK YOUR FLASHLIGHT!

"Apply thine heart unto instruction and thine ears to the words of knowledge" (Proverbs 23:12).

Our attitude toward God's instruction shows as we follow the plan He has charted out for us. We can actually do it our own way or make excuses as to why we take the detours ahead instead of following the road map. It requires our eyes, ears, *and* hearts to be able to see all that He has promised us on this journey called "life."

"My son, give me thine heart, and let thine eyes observe my ways" (Proverbs 23:26).

No need to fear the dense fog up ahead, friend, because if we willingly offer Him our hearts, our eyes will stay on the road map.

In my conference room, I have placed a large black Bible on a small white column. Its purpose is, of course, for easy access as I counsel people but most especially when I am sought for the correction of a child. It is important for children to know God early so that they may keep themselves from more trouble than is needed as they learn who God is and His purpose for their life. For you, young moms, remember: as soon as a child can talk, teach them to memorize and quote scripture. I know firsthand

SHARON LOYD *and* SHERI EDWARDS

what a blessing this will be not only for you but also for others as well.

A ten-year-old girl entered my office and sat down, staring at me as I stared back.

"So, why are you here?"

"I don't know."

"Wrong answer. Why are you here?"

"They think I stole some money, but I didn't. I found it on the cafeteria floor, but I can give it back."

"Who would you give it back to?"

"The girl who lost her money."

"Go get the Book."

I had the young girl turn to Ephesians 4:25–29, and as she read it out loud, her little eyes kept peeking above the big, black Book. It was the first time she had ever come to the principal's office. She began to cry, and I felt bad for her, but I needed her to know my God and what His Word says about liars and thieves. Sound hard to you? The Word of God keeps us in check. If we hide these pure words of our Lord, then truth cannot be known. It is there, but we may have not taken the time that day to read it. This is an awesome reality check for us all as we journey together this year. This little girl was fearful of being in my office and rightfully so. This was good. She needed to respect her authority and more importantly, God's Word. I have to ask myself from time to time, "Do you, Sharon, respect God's authority?"

As we look at getting to know God, we see that our minds can be renewed in the Spirit as we obey His words, as this little girl eventually saw. Even before someone has become a Christian, the Word of God can be quoted to them, because it is God who draws people to Himself. We hold that flashlight in our hands, and it is very important to *not* put it down (literally or just not pick it up) where we can't find it. Every journey needs a flashlight. I keep losing ours, and my husband just gives me that look! Do you ever get *that* look? God offers us His flashlight of truth as we take one step upon another. So, grab your flashlight for this journey and keep it ready for His need in you *and* for the need of others.

"Thy word is a lamp unto my feet, and a light unto my path" (Psalm 119:105). Children learn this verse very quickly. It is also a great comfort when we get stuck in the dark of life's journey. Say it out loud and be thankful for the truth that comes from obeying God's Word.

Time for a coffee break? Read again Proverbs 23:26: "My son (daughter), give me thine heart, (a volunteer act by you) and let thine eyes observe my ways." Our eyes rest on the Words as our heart grabs the truth pushing us down this path of knowing and walking with Him.

So, time for an engine check:

1. How is your attitude toward God's authority?

2. Does He have your whole heart? Is your map right side up?

3. Are you willing to give it to Him today?

4. Are you willing to share it with others today?

5. Is your flashlight packed?

Until next time, Lord willing,

Sharon

GET LOST!

"He that loveth his life shall lose it; and he that hateth his life in this world shall keep it unto life eternal" (John 12:25).

Every morning I bring my blood pressure cuff, notebook, Bible, and computer to the kitchen table. I then proceed to go get clean water from a container that we bring from town several times a week, and I make coffee. Depending on whether or not we have electricity, I either use the coffee maker or put the pot of water on the stove. Since it is summer here right now, I then go around and open windows and doors to hopefully let a cool breeze inside. I feed the dogs and cat and put laundry in my washing machine so I have time to hang it outside later to dry. It takes about an hour and a half to two hours for me to wash a load, depending on whether or not we have water. After doing these things, I pour a cup of coffee and sit down at the table and wait. What do I wait for you ask? A mouse. He or she usually comes out from under the cabinet and hastily looks at me and then jumps into the crooked cabinet door under my sink where it begins gnawing away at the floor. I have watched its relatives jump from the ceiling, windows, and out of the dog food container in the shed. It never ends. Don't bother sending me ideas for how to rid my life of them, because I have tried them all. When one rat dies, it isn't long before another is there to take its place.

Sometimes I will sit and watch that mouse and begin to cry. I will look at the broken cabinets, and the power will go out, and the wind won't blow. Before long, I have allowed it to wear on me. I begin thinking about how I wish I had a nicer place with things that matched and beautiful marble countertops instead of the cheaply made Brazilian junk that looks tired and worn. Inevitably, it is those days that I will get an e-mail from a church in the United States who would like an update, a DVD or Skype call. I have to put on my game face and act like missions is the greatest thing in the world and I am so thankful they would even consider us for their mission questionnaire to see if we are worthy of their support. And it will wear on me, even more.

It is also in those days that someone will post a picture of my daughter who is in college, and I have to fight my sadness all day, fretting that she is so far away. My other children will come and sit and talk to me. Eventually the question is asked, "When are we taking a furlough?" They want to learn to drive or go on a first date like all their friends in the States are doing. I tell them what I wished I could believe for myself on that particular day—that it is all part of our sacrifice and we have to be willing to give those things up for the souls in Brazil. Then that dumb mouse will run by again, and I will think about how much I hate my life.

I don't think that was what Jesus was talking about in John when he said, "And he that hateth his life in this world shall keep it unto life eternal." Nope, he wasn't talking about a missionary's wife and her pity party. Well, not in that sense anyway. But He is saying something straight to me that will cause me to quit bellyaching and whining.

Jesus tells us to come unto him (Matthew 11:28). He tells us to participate with Him in His work. He tells us we can find rest there, which means we don't have to work for our salvation, but we can rest in *His* finished work. But while we serve here, we shouldn't be caring about the things of this world. Sure, no one likes a mouse running around their kitchen or mismatched cabinets held up by blocks of wood. Nobody likes being without electricity or clean water or being away from family, but it is the end game that matters. One of these days all that surrounds me will be gone. My time on this earth will be past. A living mouse or a dead one really won't matter. I hope that by the time my journey here is done, I will have matured spiritually to the point that I don't waste my time feeling sorry for myself. I want to get to know God better, so I have to "hate" what keeps me from my goal. That means I have to hate my pity parties. I have to hate them so much that I will not want to have another one and keep my focus on what is worth my time but most especially His time.

Are you wasting time hating the wrong things too? You may not have a mouse running through your life, but I guarantee you, you have something else that the devil uses to irritate you. If you desire for something more than what God has given, you are keeping yourself from serving Him to your full potential. Choose to put those desires on your hate list. Lose your life here so He can gain other souls in heaven one day. He died for them and lost His life already. Who are we to do less?

> "Turn away mine eyes from beholding vanity; and quicken thou me in thy way" (Psalm 119:37).

Real joy comes the moment we take our eyes from ourselves and place them on our Savior. He is worth it all and more. Get lost in Him and you will find your way as you get to know Him better.

Until next time, Lord willing,

Sheri

FABULOUS FIGS FOR
THE FAMILY

This story and the provided scripture is a great devotional for ladies. If you have a ladies' fellowship or ladies' Bible study, use this lesson to enhance your study. My suggestion would be to have a container of figs on each table with some fig jam or fig Newtons with some salty crackers. Get your ladies involved by announcing ahead of time the facts at the end of this lesson. Allow them the opportunity to search out your facts and then to bring their own information to the table, so to speak. Add some olives and other seasonal fruit to your treats.

> "Whoso keepeth the fig tree shall eat the fruit thereof: so he that waiteth on his master shall be honoured" (Proverbs 27:18).

While reading my Bible, I sometimes wonder if a Hebrew or Greek word means the same as it does in our English language. Ever do that? Of course, *Strong's Concordance* is a good source for me to quickly check it out whether using the bound copy or going to an app on the computer. Either way, I chuckle at my discovery. Do you know what the Greek word is for "fig tree?" Are you ready? A fig tree! Don't you love it? My mind immediately took a detour even after Sheri warned us to stay on the main course and to not go off on some mouse chase. How in the world did Adam and Eve collect enough fig leaves to make an apron to cover their bodies? But that is exactly what they did according to Genesis 3:7. Read it when you get another break on this journey. There are different kinds of fig leaves because of so many varieties of fig trees. Duh! And I should have known that, but as you read you will find out what you really didn't know!

Make a right turn with me and help me get back on the right road: "Whoso keepeth the fig tree shall eat the fruit thereof: so he that waiteth on his master shall be honoured." Proverbs 27:18

My husband and I had a fig tree just about knee high that was good for nothing. So we dug it up and moved it next to our back porch. It grew a little but wasn't producing enough growth for a crop of figs, not even one hint of the fruit. I courageously walked outside one day, picked up the hoe, and began chopping around the scrawny tree gathering up a few weeds. As I threw them on the trash pile, I was so proud of myself for doing a grand ole job.

My husband met me with a scowl on his face and then began browbeating me all the way back to the fig tree. I wanted to pick up the hoe and do some chopping elsewhere but decided to pay attention to his words and not his actions. I didn't realize just how closely I had pounded the hoe around the root system of the tree! But, bless the Lord, in a few months the fig tree took off and grew higher and bigger than we anticipated which was almost too close to our back porch. I chuckle today as I imagine the tree smiling back at me as if to say, "Thank you for gathering the choking weeds, and by the way, I have a mouth full of figs waiting just for you!" I love my fig tree!

It is our responsibility to do as the Word of God teaches instead of questioning its authority every time we pick it up, or running to the preacher to complain about something we "think" the

Bible says or means. Our fruit *will* come back to us and fill us up, sometimes to overflowing! My favorite verses which hang in my office at this writing are found in John 15: 7–8: "If ye abide in me, and my words abide in you, ye shall ask what ye will, and it shall be done unto you. Herein is my Father glorified, that ye bear much fruit; so shall ye be my disciples." The abiding is exactly what it means: abide, live in, dwell, remain, wait for. The fruit will come as you stay in the Word and act on it. We pick up the Bible, we read it, dwell upon it, act on it, and afterward the fruit bearing begins because Jesus is dwelling in us, and we are dwelling in Him! Wow, what a truth! Let's get back to the road map and follow its direction.

Pick a Few Fig Facts (Say that ten times and have yourself a good laugh on this road trip)

1. Figs are mentioned over fifty times in scripture.

2. Figs were one of the seven species listed among the produce of the land God promised.

3. Figs can grow wild.

4. Jesus cursed the fig tree because it didn't produce figs. Jesus got hungry just like we do today!

5. Jesus used the example of fig trees to teach us that the end is near. Fig trees are the last to produce leaves.

6. Figs are a significant commercial crop in Israel.

7. Figs make great jam!

8. Fig trees have no blossoms on their branches. The blossom is inside the fruit.

9. Figs naturally help hold in moisture in baked goods and keep them fresher.

10. Figs were used as a training food for the early Olympic athletes, becoming the first Olympic "medal."

Until next time, Lord willing,

Sharon

ONE WAY ONLY

"And Samuel spake unto all the house of Israel, saying, If ye do return unto the LORD with all your hearts, then put away the strange gods and Ashtaroth from among you, and prepare your hearts unto the LORD, and serve him only: and he will deliver you out of the hand of the Philistines" (1 Samuel 7:3).

One weekend a few years back, my oldest daughter, Katie, came running to me with an idea. She wanted our family to throw sleeping bags into the car and take off for the day without deciding where we would go. Mark surprised me by agreeing with her. So, not wanting to be a spoilsport, I grabbed a towel, the tent and a change of clothes. I left my makeup and hot rollers and jumped in the car with everyone, and we headed off down the adventurous journey. We drove for hours in a direction we had never been, toward an unknown destination. This wouldn't sound so crazy if we had been in West Virginia or even Florida, but here we were in southern Brazil, driving along without a clue as to where we were headed.

That evening we pitched our small tent beside a clear but colorful lake not far from the ocean. I didn't sleep a wink for fear that some maniac would kill us in the middle of the night, so I tossed and turned while listening to the rain pelt the tent. Prickly thorns kept intruding on my sleep as well. Finally, I covered my feet and waited for morning. The sun eventually peeked over the horizon, and thankfully, we had survived. You would think we would have gotten the spontaneous adventure out of our systems by then, but the pioneer missionary husband that I married wanted to explore the surrounding area. We had once prayed over these places before ever moving to Brazil, so now the names on a map were more than just locations, and Mark wanted to take a look at what we missionaries fondly refer to as "the need."

Once again, we found ourselves meandering through sparsely traveled back roads and tiny towns, trying to spot churches as we headed in the general direction of home. After a while we decided that if we wanted to make it back home before dark, we would have to stop sightseeing and get on the highway where we could make good time. Mark punched in Lages to his Google Maps app on his phone and saw where we could take a shortcut and be back on the main road to our farm. If we had only known where it was going to take us, but the blue line on the phone didn't show that we were headed for a small dirt road that was precariously dug out of the side of the highest mountain pass in our state. I should have known when the pavement turned into dirt that we were in for trouble. I remember looking through the clouds at some high mountain peaks while pointing and joking, "At least we won't have to drive through those." How wrong I was. That was exactly where we ended up.

You know something? I think I have come far enough in life now that I can honestly say from experience: it never pays to take the easy road. Let's be truthful with ourselves here and not play games. How many of us actually try and seek to obey every last word that God has written for us in the Bible? Come on, don't just give me a hasty, holier-than-thou answer, be honest. We all try to fudge here and there to justify why we do some things and why we don't do others. We like those easy-looking paths, but they always lead us to trouble.

Samuel was God's man to deliver God's word to God's people. He didn't sugarcoat the message God had for them either. He told them very plainly that if they truly wanted God's help and deliverance from the Philistines, then they needed to return with *all* their hearts to the Lord, put away their secret gods, and *prepare* their hearts unto the Lord and serve *Him*.

The word "prepare" in this verse means "to stand up and set up in a direction" (*Strong's Exhaustive Concordance of the* Bible, The Old-Time Gospel Hour Edition, Hebrew and Chaldee Dictionary).

Where are we truly headed? Are we just placating our consciences by reading the Bible every morning and running through a list of prayer requests? Or are we really seeking after God, preparing our hearts, pointing them in His direction? If we are, then we aren't looking for the easy way out, or a new interesting way toward Him. Do we have secret "gods" that we need to cast off? We are to be hungering and thirsting after the one and true God. So are we? Let's point our hearts one way and one way only—*toward* God.

Our family made it through that mountain pass that day, but we feared for our lives the entire time. If you are trying to take the easy road in your Christian life, you know you are not living in freedom and peace. And you know in your heart that you aren't communing with God the way He wants to commune with you. The only way to fix it is to return to Him, His way, not your way. He says to return, with your whole heart. Want to know Him better? It takes your whole heart, friend. Are you willing to give it a try?

Until next time, Lord willing,

Sheri

PREPARING FOR
THE JOURNEY

(If you live in the South, you may have the opportunity to go "palm hunting" for your ladies if you use this story for a ladies meeting. Even the sabal (palmetto) palms are easily accessible and while you are collecting palm branches, why not cook up some swamp cabbage? Swamp cabbage can be eaten raw or cooked. We eat it both ways but during hunting season, we may cook up a huge pot of swamp cabbage seasoned with pork. Palm branches can be used in a variety of ways for ladies' meetings depending on the theme. Prepare the ladies before the meeting to do a Google search on "palms," "coconuts," and "branches." Ask them to be ready to discuss the many uses of this interesting tree and fruit.)

And when they drew nigh unto Jerusalem, and were come to Bethphage, unto the mount of Olives, then sent Jesus two disciples, Saying unto them, Go into the village over against you, and straightway ye shall find an ass tied, and a colt with her: loose them, and bring them unto me. And if any man say ought unto you, ye shall say, The Lord hath need of them; and straightway he will send them. All this was done, that it might be fulfilled which was spoken by the prophet, saying, TELL YE THE DAUGHTER OF SION, BEHOLD, THY KING COMETH UNTO

THEE, MEEK AND SITTING UPON AN ASS, AND A COLT THE
FOAL OF AN ASS. And the disciples went, and did as Jesus
commanded them. And brought the ass, and the colt, and
put on them their clothes, and they set him thereon. And
a very great multitude spread their garments in the way;
others cut down branches from the trees, and strawed
them in the way. And the multitudes that went before,
and that followed, cried, saying, Hosanna to the son of
David: Blessed is he that cometh in the name of the
Lord; Hosanna in the highest. And when he was come
into Jerusalem, all the city was moved, saying, Who is
this? And the multitude said, this is Jesus the prophet of
Nazareth of Galilee. (Matthew 21:1–11)

Traveling can be laborious at times, especially when something
goes wrong, like a flat tire, a vomiting child, or a sick husband. We
all know how needy a sick husband can be, almost as deprived as
a child! You can't look into the future of your journey and know
exactly what will happen, but rest assured, you can be for the most
part, prepared. As we journey through God's Word and get to
know Him better, we may need a pit stop every now and then to
regroup, taking care of these unexpected events. Take advantage
of these times by relaxing and soaking in all that God permits
on the journey. If you rush, you may miss that one nugget that is
needed for that particular day, and what is even more exciting is
the fact that the nugget may be needed for someone else.

Jesus always had time for people even as He prepared for His
entry. Think about it. Just one week before his death, He was
helping and healing people at every pit stop. Read again the
scripture of His triumphal entry into Jerusalem and then look
closely at Mark 11:1–10, Luke 19:29–38, and John 12:12–15.
All the Gospels tell this wonderful story of Jesus. Jerusalem

is an awesome place, and as I entered the city for the first time, my adrenalin was flowing so fast I believe I could have jumped from the bus and flown away! I kid you not. That is how I was first affected by this amazing, magnificent city! My husband went with me on my second trip to Israel and oh my goodness, I couldn't wait to share with him the fabulous entrance of Jerusalem with its luminosities and the magic that was so prevalent as we made that final turn down the winding hill to the city. All I could think about was Jesus on that special donkey as the people quietly laid down the palm branches while others literally spread their garments in the way. As we get to know Him, we understand God's passion for us! Everything had to be perfect, exact, because God already knew what we did not know at that time in history. He has prepared us for our journey, and, yes, that might include a vomiting child, a death, a flat tire, or financial reversal, but God has thrown down the prepared palms for us as He guides us in this journey called life. Do you understand that?

> "Blessed be he that cometh in the name of the Lord: we have blessed you out of the house of the Lord" (Psalm 118: 26).

Did you know that the palm tree represents peace and plenty? May the weights (burdens, trials) that are put upon us make us thrive all the more for the Lord Jesus Christ! Are you carrying a heavy weight today? Will you trust Him and get to know Him even more with this heavy load? I live in Florida and get to see many palms, but I've never seen Colombia's palm trees with the tallest measuring up to 197 feet. There are so many varieties of palms that would make for a grand study, don't you think? Oh my! Does it make you want to pick up God's Word and read more? There is so much in this journey to knowing God and as we climb higher, the more we can realize His greatness. He loves us! He loves us! Did you hear His words?

Until next time, Lord willing,

Sharon

THE STRONGEST ROCK
IN THE UNIVERSE

Stop and take the time to read the following passages:

"From the end of the earth will I cry unto thee, when my heart is overwhelmed: lead me to the rock that is higher than I" (Psalm 61:2).

"And he said unto me, My grace is sufficient for thee: for my strength is made perfect in weakness. Most gladly therefore will I rather glory in my infirmities, that the power of Christ may rest upon me" (2 Corinthians 12:9).

"Now the God of hope fill you with all joy and peace in believing, that ye may abound in hope, through the power of the Holy Ghost" (Romans 15:13).

"For the kingdom of God is not in word, but in power" (1 Corinthians 4:20).

"But unto them which are called, both Jews and Greeks, Christ the power of God, and the wisdom of God" (1 Corinthians 1:24).

Mark and I once caught a bus in Paris that conveyed us to the beaches of Normandy. As we arrived at our destination, I felt a deep sense of appreciation settle in my heart for my papa, who fought on the front lines in Germany during World War II. My heart saluted him and the many others, including my dad, my father-in-law, and my own husband, who have proudly donned a uniform for our country.

During our trip, we wandered through old bunkers along the cliffs of the English Channel. It was truly a beautiful site, but I tried to imagine what the view must have been like to the young soldiers in June of 1944. The Channel would have been filled with ships, cannons would have been exploding, and soldiers would have been crying out amid the rapid gunfire. It must have been surreal as they sought shelter from the hail of bullets that descended on them from the German soldiers. Honestly, I don't think I will ever have a clue at how scary those hours must have truly been.

At one point, we climbed down a steep embankment until our feet were standing on Omaha Beach. Mark and I both fought tears, knowing we were standing where the blood of many a mother's son had soaked the sand all those years ago. I heard a few children laughing as they built sand castles and dug into the beach. At first I felt a little irritated by their joy at such a solemn spot, but then I realized their cheerfulness was proof of their freedom, purchased by the lives of those who had fought there. I removed my shoes and wandered down the beach, thanking God for what I so often have taken for granted.

One spot of the World War II battlefronts we visited was a place called Pointe Du Hoc. It was there on June 6, 1944, that 225 Rangers commenced their mission to take back ground from the Germans, but doing so meant climbing sheer rocky cliffs. Two days into their battle, 135 Rangers had either been killed or wounded, but the ninety men who were left kept going. When one Ranger fell, another immediately took his spot. These men were determined to take back that highpoint from the enemy, and in the end, they were victorious. By doing so, they valiantly recovered an area of France where the Allied armies could continue pushing back at Hitler's Nazi regime.

Pointe Du Hoc had been free at one time, but the enemy had chosen to use the strength and position of the land against the Allied forces. But it was the strength and position of that very land that helped the Rangers climb and attain their victory. The Rangers shot rope ladders into the rocks and climbed them until they reached the top and advanced head on with the enemy. A memorial stands there today, representing the daggers of the Rangers, reminding all that see it of their success.

This reminds me all too well of our Rock, Jesus Christ. And it reminds me of how every day the devil misuses God's Word in our lives. He twists it and turns it until we are shaking in our boots, afraid we are not doing right or that we are unworthy to serve the Lord. He started in the garden of Eden with Eve and twisted what God had said. He used the strength and position of the truth, twisted it into a lie, and Eve fell for it. If she had only stopped long enough to think, really think, what God had truly said, she might have just shoved that forbidden fruit in Satan's face and told him to go choke on it.

Who is our God? He is not an amulet to be carried around to bring us luck or bless us. He is God. He is a Rock, a refuge, and a shelter.

> "But the Lord is my defence; and my God is the rock of my refuge" (Psalm 94:22).

> "From the end of the earth will I cry unto thee, when my heart is overwhelmed: lead me to the rock that is higher than I" (Psalm 61:2).

The Bible calls God our Rock.

> "For who is God save the Lord? or who is a rock save our God?" (Psalm 18:31)

The Bible names Jesus as that Rock.

> "And did all drink the same spiritual drink: for they drank of that spiritual Rock that followed them: and that Rock was Christ" (1 Corinthians 10:4).

We can seek shelter there, we can hide from the fire of the enemy there, and we can rest there. The strength and the position of our Rock is like none other. We can trust in Him at all times.

In 1984, President Ronald Reagan gave a speech at Pointe Du Hoc to the very Rangers who fought to secure that ground in World War II. He posed the question, "Why? Why did you do it? What impelled you to put aside the instinct for self-preservation and risk your lives to take these cliffs? What inspired all the men of the armies that met here?" He continued and answered for them, "It was faith and belief; it was loyalty and love."

I echo those words to you, my friend. The enemy may be shooting at you from way up high, and it would appear that God is not helping you, or even listening to your prayers, but you must remind yourself of the truth and not be led to believe the lie of the enemy. You must have faith and a belief that God is not mocked by the enemy, nor does He wiggle in His boots at the thought of the enemy. God is the Rock. He is unmovable, unshakeable, and unchangeable, and He will lend you His strength and enable you with His power to wage through the battle you are currently facing.

God will shelter you when you are getting too weak to move forward. God will send you help in your time of despair. God will pull you up with His mighty right hand when you feel as though you are going to fall, but you have got to keep your eyes on Him. We must not let the enemy deceive us into thinking God is a liar and all hope is lost. It is quite the opposite!

> "That by two immutable things, in which it was impossible for God to lie, we might have a strong consolation, who have fled for refuge to lay hold upon the hope set before us: Which hope we have as an anchor of the soul, both sure and stedfast, and which entereth into that within the veil" (Hebrews 6:18–19).

Are you getting so tired in the battle that you are shutting down? Are you believing the devil when he whispers, "God doesn't care"? Well, let me tell you something: This is not the time to quit reading your Bible. This is not the time to quit praying. This is not the time to quit in general. This is the time to dig in with the sword of the truth and continue to take back ground that the enemy wants you to believe is gone. It isn't.

You and I have paused today on our journey for some sightseeing. We are looking at the magnificence that is our God. He is our shelter in the time of storm. He is strong enough for us to lean on and He will hold us up.

> "For in the time of trouble he shall hide me in his pavilion: in the secret of his tabernacle shall he hide me; he shall set me up upon a rock" (Psalm 27:5)

You may be facing a day full of problems. Matter of truth, your life may just be a mess right now, and you may be partly to blame. But God has not abandoned you, my friend. Put your phone, tablet, or computer aside and get somewhere that you can call on your Rock. Confess anything that may be hindering your communication with Him. Humble yourself in His sight and tell

Him you are seeking shelter. You need his strength, or you will not make it. Continue all day long looking up and asking Him to keep you steady and on His solid ground. Listen for when He says to move and, most definitely, stop when He says to stop. He will not fail you.

When God does give you the victory, testify of it to others. Leave your memorial there on the Rock for all to see that it is God who gives the victory. It is God who remained steadfast when all else was lost. Reach down and help another as they climb. Don't cut their ropes. Advance and continue. Have faith and believe that the next battle can be fought and won, just like the last, as long as you keep your eyes on the Rock.

This concludes this part of our tour. I hope you have enjoyed seeing the strongest Rock in the universe.

Until next time, Lord willing,

Sheri

THERE MAY BE A HUNGRY LION AHEAD!

If at all possible, try and read Daniel 6: 1–28. Surely, we all can stop for a minute and read this most popular account of the faithful Daniel who stays true to the ways of God and yet has been accused of wrongdoing.

Have you ever been falsely accused of something and found yourself in a predicament? I have, more than once. Daniel's decision to worship God has been challenged, thus making him appear the enemy of the king. What an excellent book for young boys and young men to study, memorizing portions for the road ahead which may be full of temptation. Getting to know Daniel is a step closer to getting to know our God, because everything Daniel did was a reflection of his God.

> "Then this Daniel was preferred above the presidents and princes, because an excellent spirit was in him; and the king thought to set him over the whole realm. Then the presidents and princes sought to find occasion against Daniel concerning the kingdom; but they could find none occasion nor fault; forasmuch as he was faithful, neither was there any error or fault found in him. Then said these men, We shall not find any occasion against this Daniel, except we find it against him concerning the law of his God" (Daniel 6:3–5).

Even King Darius believed in Daniel, not his God, but in him, as a man and leader. The Bible records this faith in verse 16, "Then the king commanded, and they brought Daniel, and cast him into the den of lions. Now the king spake and said unto Daniel, Thy God whom thou servest continually, he will deliver thee." Daniel had been thrown into the lion's den. Did you get that? King Darius believed that Daniel's God would deliver him.

I wonder if people who do not know the Savior have that kind of confidence in us as we live for God, working side by side with them, shopping with them, and serving with them in the local church. Do we point people to the cross, or are we hypocrites trying to live a double life to please all people? Daniel was a man full of integrity and exemplified the great God. Oh, I fear at the judgment that God will look at me and say some things that I surely dread to hear. Yes, our sins are forgiven, but so many times we have consequences that follow those forgiven sins. On this journey to know Him, we must realize that God cannot lie and will not tolerate unrighteous living. He loves us and so desires for us to "be ye Holy as I am Holy," even to being thrown to the lions in full confidence in His will for our lives.

Praise the Lord for Daniel's faith in God. He could have just done as the decree proclaimed, but he, very quietly but not secretly, continued to bow and worship God as the Bible records in verse 10, "Now when Daniel knew that the writing was signed, he went into his house; and his windows being open in his chamber toward Jerusalem, he kneeled upon his knees three times a day, and prayed, and gave thanks before his God, as he did aforetime."

In this journey to knowing God, stop and pull over thinking about this. Even King Darius stated to Daniel that he believed God would deliver him, but when he sheepishly went to the den the next morning, verse 20 states, "He cried with a lamentable voice unto Daniel: and the king spake and said to Daniel, O Daniel, servant of the living God, is thy God, whom thou servest continually, able to deliver thee from the lions?"

People watch us closely sometimes, to falsely accuse us or to trap us but at other times to see what we will actually do when the lions are at our front door! In this journey, we face the enemy, but we must realize that we serve a real, live God who is greater than that enemy and He controls the mouth of the lion! Never should we address Satan for fear that he may answer us. Tell God because He is the one in control of all, even ole slew foot!

One last pit stop to think about—these jealous, greedy men (you do realize that people may be jealous of you) set out to do evil, but evil came back much more heavily on them than did the damage they sought for Daniel. I cry in my spirit as I read the account in verse 24, "And the king commanded, and they brought those men which had accused Daniel, and they cast them into the den of lions, them, their children, and their wives; and the lions had the mastery of them, and brake all their bones in pieces or ever they came at the bottom of the den."

Did you get that? These precious wives and children had to die at the mouths of the lions because of the sin of their dad and husband! To the living God that we would live righteously before our husbands, our children, and grandchildren for fear that they will be destroyed by our foolish decisions! Consequences face us, but we must still continue to read, study, learn, and reproduce this living Word of our Lord!

Until next time, Lord willing!

Sharon

DON'T GET KIDNAPPED!

"Only take heed to thyself, and keep thy soul diligently, lest thou forget the things which thine eyes have seen, and lest they depart from thy heart all the days of thy life: but teach them thy sons, and thy sons' sons" (Deuteronomy 4:9).

"I said, I will take heed to my ways, that I sin not with my tongue: I will keep my mouth with a bridle, while the wicked is before me" (Psalm 39:1).

"Watch and pray, that ye enter not into temptation: the spirit indeed is willing, but the flesh is weak" (Matthew 26:41).

On two separate occasions in my life, someone has tried to kidnap me: Once when I was just a little girl in a department store and once as an adult while on the mission field. Both were frightening experiences and have made me a paranoid mother. I am hypervigilant of strangers approaching me and my children, and rarely do I go anywhere without one of my sons or my husband beside me. I just don't want to ever have that "trapped" feeling again.

Last week one of our college girls at our church here in Brazil was kidnapped at gunpoint while getting into her car at the beach.

Thankfully the intoxicated teenagers were just wanting the car and let her go a little while later, but the incident has troubled her so much that she jumps at the slightest noise, and she is fearful to be alone.

We all have been warned by our parents to "stay close" and "don't wander off." I am sure you are thinking of a frightening time in your own past where you or your child was in a dangerous situation. It is an awful feeling, isn't it? After you "lose" a child in a busy store or library, your heart is pounding and horrifying images run through your brain at a million miles per second. Once you finally have them in your arms, you promise yourself it will never happen again. You turn into a watchdog in the grocery store. Your kids roll their eyes when you yell out their names as they linger by the candy aisle. But slowly you forget that chilling feeling. Slowly your defenses come down, and before too long, you don't even notice when they have run off to put quarters in the claw machine at the department store.

Isn't it the same way in our spiritual lives? The devil leads us off with a sweet piece of candy that seems harmless, and it is too late when we feel the effects from what was really inside the wrapper—death to our prayer lives, death to our Bible readings, and death to our service at the church. And it was all because we wanted to "check Facebook quickly" before our time alone with our Savior.

We forget to be watchful of any little thing that gets between us and our Lord. Or maybe we decided to let an argument here and a quarrel there come between us and our spouse instead of keeping that communication open. Before long we are laughing too much and staring too long in the eyes of someone who didn't put the ring on our finger. The so-called candy that Satan had nicely wrapped up for us was full of poison and death. God wasn't joking when He told us in James 1:15, "Then when lust hath conceived, it bringeth forth sin: and sin, when it is finished, bringeth forth death."

Satan wants to kidnap you. He wants to hold your thoughts, your desires, and your heart captive. He wants to destroy you, and he will do whatever it takes to lead you away from where God wants you to be. The same free will you exercised to repent and turn to God as your Lord and Savior is the same free will that you can use to flee from the evil one. Don't dilly-dally around with whatever it is he is tempting you with right now. Your spiritual life is *not* worth it.

Jesus paid the ransom for you already. He wants you to get to know *Him* better and it is up to you just how far you will yield to temptation or how close you will snuggle up to our awe-inspiring God. I challenge you today to take inventory of your life, not how others see it, not how you wish it was, but a good, hard, and honest evaluation of every part of your walk with God. Are you saved? If so, are you vigilant about keeping that relationship current with your Father? Have you talked to Him today? He is there and will shelter you from the tempter with a way of escape.

- Flee from evil.

- Sound the alarm in your soul.

- Don't get kidnapped!

"Wherefore let him that thinketh he standeth take heed lest he fall" (1 Corinthians 10:12).

Until next time, Lord willing,

Sheri

THE TONGUE THAT
NEVER STOPS!

"Keep thy foot when thou goest to the house of God, and be more ready to hear, than to give the sacrifice of fools: for they consider not that they do evil. Be not rash with thy mouth, and let not thine heart be hasty to utter any thing before God: for God is in heaven, and thou upon earth: therefore let thy words be few. For a dream cometh through the multitude of business; and a fool's voice is known by multitude of words" (Ecclesiastes 5:1–3).

There's nothing quite like a person, whether a child or adult, who just will not shut his or her mouth long enough for someone else to get a word in the conversation, especially on a road trip. Would you agree? You are stuck and the wagging tongue goes on and on and on. Oh me!

A dear Christian friend of mine came to me one Sunday after church seeking some help with a particular problem, and I asked her this question, "What has God already said about this problem?"

She looked a little surprised when I asked her, and she tried to avoid the question by talking over me. Finally, I touched her arm and said, "Stop. What has God already instructed you about it?"

"What do you mean? I don't know what He has said. That is the reason I am asking you!"

"Sit down, and let's find out what He has given us in His Word." I already knew what God had written about the matter, but I needed for her to see the convicting words of the Lord. Her heart needed to be changed, and I couldn't do that, but God's Word could.

Once we read the scriptures together and talked a few minutes she asked, "How did you know that, Sharon?" I just sat there staring at her and said, "Because I have already read that before today."

Seeing that this dear lady, who appeared to know God and His Word, really didn't, I had to back up and park for a few minutes. "Talk to me about your devotions, you know, your time alone with God."

With her head bowed, her eyes looked down at the floor, and she quietly said, "I just don't have time, Sharon, with work, the children, and my husband." I have seen that look a thousand times it seems from women who have time for everything else but God. Then, she said with a little gleam in her eyes, "I pray a lot."

"Oh, so you admit that you talk a lot to God, but you don't have time for Him to talk back to you. Is that right?"

We both began to laugh! Thank goodness she was not offended. "Talk to me about your day," I said.

She did and we found approximately thirty minutes in the morning before she began breakfast for the children. It was rewarding to see this precious mom trying to plan a time alone with her God. At one point she admitted that she used to get up earlier and read someone else's devotion but got discouraged in trying to do everything the writer instructed. "Why don't you just begin by reading the Bible through, you know, chapter by chapter?" I suggested.

"You mean the entire Bible!"

"No, just a couple of chapters or more a day, and maybe in a year you could have the whole Bible read."

"Oh, I never could do that! It is too hard, and besides, I don't understand the Old Testament," she exclaimed.

"What part do you not understand?" I asked.

"Well, all of it!" She laughed.

"You've never read the Old Testament, have you?"

She laughed again and said, "No, but I have looked at it, and it seems too difficult." We talked some more, and she began to see that she just needed to get started. She had listened to the devil long enough. It was time for her to quit giving him her ear.

I said, "You know, you've admitted to talking to God but haven't picked up His Words for Him to talk back to you. You also admitted to me tonight that you have taken time to listen to the enemy, and you have believed his lies. It's time to shut his mouth by the words in this Book, the Bible, believing the truth and start living a life full of joy, peace, and happiness. Don't you think?"

If you study Psalm 119, you will find so many beautiful nuggets of truth. Your life will begin to shine with brightness as you take this journey with us. Ponder these thoughts, these words of absolute truth, if you truly want to know God better today than you did yesterday.

PSALM 119

- 🖋 11—Thy word have I hid in mine heart, that I might not sin against thee.

- 🖋 50—This is my comfort in my affliction: for thy word hath quickened me.

- 🖋 97—O how love I thy law! It is my meditation all the day.

- 🖋 103—How sweet are thy words unto my taste! yea, sweeter than honey to my mouth!

- 🖋 105—Thy word is a lamp unto my feet, and a light unto my path.

God desires to hear from us, but He also yearns to be heard! Why not, on this road trip to knowing God, take the time to close your mouth and listen to Him. Pick up the Book and say, "Good morning, Lord. What are you going to say to me today? I am listening, Lord!" If you have a plan and are walking with God, maybe it is time to share it with someone. Ask God to place that person in your path. If you struggle in this area, and we all do at some time in our lives, then read with me of a simple but powerful plan that may just work for you.

These five simple but powerful scriptures from Psalm 119 can be used in a ladies' Bible study simply by planning ahead and asking some of your ladies who have seen the scriptures come alive in their own families to testify to the truth of God's Word. Ask them to be prepared to share, but always remember you may have to give them a specific time limit or else you may have someone who does not know when to "shut her own mouth."

Until next time, Lord willing,

Sharon

LANDMARK

Have you ever wanted God to just—*poof!*—appear before you and tell you what is really going on in your life? I have. I can think of numerous times when I have been praying and weeping, snot running down my face, tears streaming out of my eyes, no words coming out of my mouth, but begging in my mind with a prayer similar to this: "God, please let me know that you are listening! Do you hear me God? Do you see me? I can't take anymore! Please help me."

It is absolutely distressing when you finally stand up after praying like that and all you get in return is a deafening silence. Your mind starts to wonder if the writers of the song "He Knows My Name" even knew what they were talking about.

"If He knows my name, why isn't He hearing my prayer?" you sarcastically comment to yourself. Then you begin to make deals with Him and ask for a sign. Maybe it is a butterfly, a rainbow, or in my case, a woodpecker. You are so desperate for confirmation of His ability to hear your prayers that you will do anything to convince yourself that He hears and sees you. But He emphasizes it quite clearly in both the Old Testament and New Testament that He hears you.

> "The eyes of the LORD are upon the righteous, and his ears are open unto their cry" (Psalm 34:15).

"For the eyes of the Lord are over the righteous, and his ears are open unto their prayers: but the face of the Lord is against them that do evil" (1 Peter 3:12).

Life can find us in some pretty hard spots, let me tell you. There we are living our lives, serving the Lord, and then out of nowhere, *bam!* We are in the middle of a mess, and we never saw it approaching. Nothing makes sense. our faith we sang about in church on Sunday dwindles to nothing as we begin to question everything.

I am writing this today on our journey, because none of us knows what the coming months may bring. And we need to place a landmark here that we can return to when we doubt whether or not God is paying any attention to us. When He chooses to be silent, it will be for a reason, a perfect reason, and we will just need to trust and believe what His Word says is enough. God has made us some promises, and He will *not* go back on them. Let's list some, and when you forget, or just feel as though you are all alone and no one cares, come back here. Come back and read the truth.

"O Lord, thou hast searched me, and known me. Thou knowest my downsitting and mine uprising, thou understandest my thought afar off. Thou compassest my path and my lying down, and art acquainted with all my ways. For there is not a word in my tongue, but, lo, O Lord, thou knowest it altogether. Thou hast beset me behind and before, and laid thine hand upon me. Such knowledge is too wonderful for me; it is high, I cannot attain unto it" (Psalm 139:1–6).

1. He sees me when I sit down and when I get up.

2. He hears every word I speak.

3. He is before me and behind me.

"The eyes of the LORD are in every place, beholding the evil and the good" (Proverbs 15:3).

4. He sees the evil as well as the good. He is everywhere all the time.

"Be strong and of a good courage, fear not, nor be afraid of them: for the LORD thy God, he it is that doth go with thee; he will not fail thee, nor forsake thee" (Deuteronomy 31:6).

5. He goes with me and will never forsake me.

"For the LORD will not cast off his people, neither will he forsake his inheritance" (Psalm 94:14).

"For I know the thoughts that I think toward you, saith the LORD, thoughts of peace, and not of evil, to give you an expected end" (Jeremiah 29:11).

6. His thoughts are on me constantly for my good and not for evil. I can trust Him.

"Let your conversation be without covetousness; and be content with such things as ye have: for he hath said, I will never leave thee, nor forsake thee" (Hebrews 13:5).

You may not feel it, but God is watching. He sees you when you get yourself in a jam because of your sinful nature, and He will call your attention to it. He sees when someone else makes your life miserable, and He knows it hurts you, and He will not leave you to suffer alone. Even in the most unfair of situations, He bends His ear and listens while your nose runs, your eyes are raw from crying, and you are without real words. He listens to your heart. You don't need a sign, and you don't need His audible voice if you will just believe He is who He says He is. Run to Him, dwell in His presence, and let Him show you just how much He can do.

This process of getting to know Him will call for such a time as this. Don't quit! Remember to

- stop;

- turn around; and

- run to the landmark where truth abides.

Until next time, Lord willing,

Sheri

SAME PLACE, SAME TIME, AND SAME BIBLE

"For ever, O Lord, thy word is settled in heaven" (Psalm 119:89).

"But the word of the Lord endureth for ever. And this is the word which by the gospel is preached unto you" (1 Peter 1:25).

"Cause me to hear thy lovingkindness in the morning; for in thee do I trust: cause me to know the way wherein I should walk; for I lift up my soul unto thee" (Psalm 143:8).

While talking to a dear friend who was desperately struggling in an area of her life, I asked her this question, "How is it with you and God each day? Tell me about your private devotions."

She replied, "Well, my husband and I read the Bible together. We are in the Old Testament," and she named the book and then continued to share with me the most beautiful time each morning where this couple met God and shared the Word together.

Then I asked her some more questions, realizing that this dear friend may not have a one-on-one personal time with God. She loved to pray and write down her prayer requests, but most of the time even that prayer time was led by her husband. Her relationship with God was lacking, and I needed to find out why. She really didn't have an alone time. She admitted that she had tried to read by herself but for many reasons became discouraged as she gave an ear to the enemy. Her alone time with God became "just her talking" to Him.

I asked her this question: "What color are your husband's eyes?"

"Blue, of course!"

"Do you know his favorite food?"

She was beginning to feel uncomfortable but replied, "Now, Sharon, you know I do."

I continued, "Okay, how much time are you spending with him each day?"

Now she was beginning to see more clearly.

"Sounds like you have a really good relationship with your husband, but you are missing a great blessing by not having an alone time, yourself, you know, just you and God."

She agreed, and as we smiled at each other, she admitted, "I pray but I don't give God time to talk, do I?"

I shook my head in agreement and explained to her that if she talked all the time to her husband and didn't give him time to respond, he probably wouldn't be as patient with her as God had been all these years. It was good for us to laugh together as I saw my dear friend understand that she had a responsibility to meet God, alone, each day. Our God is a longsuffering heavenly Father!

She needed a plan for her walk with God. How are you doing?

I have shared the following plan with numerous friends, and it will help you *if* you need a kick in your step or a kick somewhere else!

1. Same Place: Choose a place of least resistance for interruptions. I love our back porch. We live in the country, and I am blessed with singing birds, playful squirrels, and sometimes a hungry coyote, but always with God. Maybe you have to lock yourself up in the bathroom, because you found that your children will at least leave you alone there for a few minutes. Just look around your home and ask God to help you see a place to meet Him every day. As I grew up reading the Bible, especially as a teen, I had to slip down to the Anthony cemetery. There were so many children in our home back then with no place for a quiet spot. My parents were not Christians at that time and didn't understand the need for private devotions. The cemetery worked for me. I know it sounds morbid, but at least I didn't have to worry about someone bothering me. Same place. Do you have it?

2. Same Time: Choose a time, same time, and every day if at all possible. My time is 5:00 a.m. and sometimes sooner, depending on my schedule for that day. I realize you may not have that privilege. No one is grading your time either. Remember that! You are in control of your time; now choose it. Some women like the evening. I can't wait until then, because my body is worn out. The day has ended, and I have to have that fresh walk with God early. But maybe your work schedule fluctuates. Remember: God doesn't sleep! Look at your time and ask God to help you choose His time to speak to you through His Word. Same time! Have you picked your time?

3. Same Bible: Use the same Bible for your devotions, your personal walk with God. Keep a journal with your Bible and be ready to write down what He tells you, personally, just for you. I like the ones with a spiral so I can fold them back and place in my Bible. Many department stores sell them for under five dollars. I have kept journals for years now. Writing is therapy for me and a way to express myself to God and Him to me. Some people like their computers and have the Bible downloaded on it. That's their choice. I like to hold God's Word in my hand, underlining passages that jump out at me. My Bible is very personal to me. The color, the smell, the pages, it's just personal, folks. It is life and death to me. As I read, I like to write down stuff in the margins of my Bible and date it. That way, as I finish the Bible for the year, I am reminded of God's goodness and His answers to prayer the next year while reading the same passage. It's new every morning, friend, and needed like that first glass of water or cup of coffee in the morning. I need to hear God all the time! Same Bible! Do you have a good ole King James Version?

There are several Bible reading plans written by many wonderful men and women. Write me and I will send you a plan that only takes thirty-six weeks to finish the entire Bible! Just think, every word of God every year can be read, but no one is grading you. No one is following you around, making sure you cross off your chapters. This is your time alone with God. Remember: you are learning more and more about this great God of ours, and what better way to know Him than just opening His mouth, in the same place, at the same time using the same Bible.

Until next time, Lord willing,

Sharon

WALKING THE WATERLINES

"No man also seweth a piece of new cloth on an old garment: else the new piece that filled it up taketh away from the old, and the rent is made worse. And no man putteth new wine into old bottles: else the new wine doth burst the bottles, and the wine is spilled, and the bottles will be marred: but new wine must be put into new bottles" (Mark 2:21–22).

"Because thine heart was tender, and thou hast humbled thyself before the LORD, when thou heardest what I spake against this place, and against the inhabitants thereof, that they should become a desolation and a curse, and hast rent thy clothes, and wept before me; I also have heard thee, saith the LORD" (2 Kings 22:19).

"All scripture is given by inspiration of God, and is profitable for doctrine, for reproof, for correction, for instruction in righteousness: That the man of God may be perfect, throughly furnished unto all good works" (2 Timothy 3:16–17).

Our family serves the Lord as missionaries in the mountains of southern Brazil. We currently rent a large farm where we grow our own vegetables and raise enough cattle to stock the freezer with meat for the year. Our church is about twenty-five kilometers away inside the city of Lages. Many people ask us why we live so far from town. No, we are not "preppers" or extremists. Our decision to live this way was made mainly for our children. We wanted them to know how to work and care for their future families. They have learned how to care for sheep, cattle, and chickens as well as plow and plant a garden. They know how to live without constant electricity, no heat or air conditioning, and keep the wood stove going. But one thing has proven to be a real big, fat pain in the neck out here, and that is water.

Our water comes from a natural spring up the hill from us. Each surrounding farm has lines that run through a barrel-filter system and then to their houses. The lines for our house run quite a way through pastures, meadows, and streams. The pipes are not completely buried in some parts, and all it takes is one cow walking by to squash a section, and we are subsequently without water until the leak is found and repaired.

In my backyard I have a fountain that is constantly running, because it is an overflow of our house's water system. As long as that fountain is going strong, I know I can do the laundry, cook, and shower with no problem, but in the middle of the night, if I hear it stop, I know we are out of water. Would you like to know how often that fountain stops running? Every. Single. Stinking. Day! Yep, as I mentioned earlier, big, fat pain in the neck.

Our boys get sick of walking the waterlines. Sometimes after fixing a break by using cut up pieces of inner tubes, they have to walk all the way to the top where the water starts, then open the air lines along the way, then walk all the way back to close them. Sometimes I try and fix the problem myself and open the lines near the house and let the air out, but it doesn't always work. I have to call the boys and send them up the hill with their boots and tools to take care of the job.

This past weekend we couldn't figure out what was causing the water to fail. I let the air out of the lines around the house. We checked the pipes under the water tank and still didn't have any water. Mark and I walked out by the barn and saw some standing water, found a loose pipe, and fixed it, but it still didn't resolve the problem. The boys walked the line and found two small breaks, but still we couldn't get the fountain going. I don't have to tell you how exasperated I was or how much I would have liked to take a hoe to the whole entire system. Finally, we found another loose pipe, let the air out again, and voila, we had water filling the tanks and dishes could be washed, and no one would go to church smelling like yesterday.

I asked God to show me what He was trying to teach me through these water problems. Patience? Trust? Hard work? I just wanted to be aware if He was trying to tell me something. I sat down with my Bible and read over my Sunday school lesson, and the Holy Spirit quickly began showing me truth and worked in my heart. My lesson was on King Josiah. Do you remember the boy who became king of Judah at eight years of age? He walked with the Lord and did that which was right according to the scriptures. He wanted his people to clean up the Temple, and during their repairs, they found the Book of the Law. Josiah couldn't believe what he heard when Shapan the Scribe read it to him. He had it read to the people, and they began taking action to obey the Words written in the scrolls. Why? Because King Josiah had wanted to make needed repairs, and he had found where the real problem was, lack of truth and obedience of that truth.

These aggravating water problems here on the farm are the result of cheap pipes that have been patched over one too many times.

Also, the cheap pipes are not properly buried. They are left exposed to whatever wants to break them, be it the heat from the sun, a big heavy heifer, or a hailstorm. The solution is for the owner to dig new lines, lay new pipe, and cover them properly. Our daily patch jobs were not working and certainly were not the solution!

Jesus spoke of Judaism and Christianity in the New Testament, comparing it to putting new cloth on old garments because the hole could end up being bigger in the end. The principle is the same with our spiritual lives. We shouldn't keep patching it up. We need to walk the lines of our heart and make sure there are not major repairs to be made. These old pipes that keep breaking around here on the farm are worthless; the patches are temporary and sometimes the "fixes" cause other weaker parts to burst. If you and I are not careful, we will just clean up for Sunday morning church or to teach our Sunday school class and not really ever get down to where the real problem is that keeps us from a fruitful walk with our Lord. And when the storms and trials come, we are left exposed, weak, and ready to break.

We want to get to know Him better, right? Well, He wants the same thing. He wants us to enjoy life living in the Spirit, not constantly working and patching in the flesh. Wouldn't it be a real peace bringer in your life if you sat down with God and let Him walk the lines of your heart with you? He has everything that you need in His Word. He has given you all the tools to really live for Him, walk with Him, and serve Him. Just like I have all the water in the world from that spring at the top of the hill, but I can't use it if I have cracked pipes. The Word of God is what will furnish us with what we need, and it will show us where to make the repairs in our relationship with Him, but we have to read it. Same time, same place, same Bible.

This is a simple illustration from everyday life, but one that I hope makes an impression on all of us. If we will just take that daily inventory with the Lord, we can find life a lot easier to live in Him. When the storms come, we won't be worried that they will break us; we will know the line is secure. When that big, fat heifer of a sister in Christ comes with her loose lips and cutting words, we won't even let it get under our skin, because we will know the lines are strong and secure. We will be equipped to help her and not get aggravated with her. When the enemy shoots those fiery darts at us, we will keep right on going and serving because we know God has everything cared for in every area of our lives.

Go walk your lines with Him.

Until next time, Lord willing,

Sheri

LET'S GET A PLAN

"Open thou mine eyes, that I may behold wondrous things out of thy law" (Psalm 119:18).

"But thou, when thou prayest, enter into thy closet, and when thou hast shut thy door, pray to thy Father which is in secret; and thy Father which seeth in secret shall reward thee openly" (Matthew 6:6).

"Surely the righteous shall give thanks unto thy name: the upright shall dwell in thy presence" (Psalm 140:13).

"I exhort therefore, that, first of all, supplications, prayers, intercessions, and giving of thanks, be made for all men" (1 Timothy 2:1).

As a young mother trying to figure out all things for all people, I struggled in getting my priorities in order. God blessed me with a wonderful pastor, Brother Gene Keith, of Countryside Baptist Church in Gainesville, Florida. He and his lovely wife, Teulah, were my lifelines back in those early days of motherhood. Brother Gene and Miss Teulah were a unique couple and had a gift for compassionate teaching to people, especially couples. I admired this elderly couple (they were only in their forties at the time!) and paid close attention to Brother Gene's daily broadcast of "The Sound of Inspiration."

Each day I grabbed my notebook and Bible to write down the scriptures he used as he taught God's Word. After joining the ladies' Bible study, I learned more about God and discovered the 959 Plan. In short the plan taught us how to pray in nine minutes and fifty-nine seconds followed by a Bible study. Brother Gene wrote the study and then printed out questions to answer.

My first entry in my notebook was dated November 19, 1973. I have kept these teachings and used them over and over throughout my life. The old blue notebook is worn, but certainly the words are as fresh to my soul as the day I heard them! Thank God for this plan. If you struggle as a young mom and feel like you just can't get over the hump, you may desire to consider this simple plan. There are six divisions which I have listed below:

1. Prayer of praise: Praise God for all He has done for you today and in the past,

2. Prayer of thanksgiving: Thank Him for answered prayer and for His goodness.

3. Prayer of confession: Confess your sins and make things right with Him and others.

4. Prayer of intercession: Pray for others and their needs. Write those dates down.

5. Prayer of petition: Ask God for what you need, not necessarily for what you want be thankful for what you do have.

6. Prayer of silence: Be still and listen to the still small voice of God. Quote memorized Scriptures.

It is very important to pray before beginning your Bible study, whether using the 959 Plan or other plans. Talking to God gets your mind in touch with His Holy Spirit. Now you are ready to listen to God. May I share this story with you?

The phone rang. "Mrs. Loyd, do you have a minute?" I listened to one of our sweet, young mom's cry for help as she poured her heart out to me, seeking advice for an emergency in their family.

"Are you able to get to my office right now?" She did and we got on our knees before the living God and opened His Word to see what He had already said about this kind of situation. It was very clear what she needed to do. She saw it and I encouraged her to do as the scriptures said. We prayed again, trusting that God had heard us. We left it there but got up from our knees and began talking. I needed to see where she was in her walk with God.

"So, tell me about your day. How are the children?" She explained how difficult life was for her right now, but she was making progress, handling the troubles one at a time.

"What are you learning in your Bible study right now? How is your walk with God?"

With that same tilted head I had seen many, many times, she answered, "I am tired all the time from work, the children, and the ministry. I just don't have the time to read all those chapters Pastor Andy told us about."

"All those chapters? Oh, you mean the Read the Bible Through in a Year?"

"Yes. It's just too much."

"That is just a guide. No one is grading you. No one is standing over your shoulder. You just cross off a chapter when you read it. It doesn't matter how many. At the end of it all, you will have read the entire Bible. Who cares how long it takes?"

"But I don't understand the Bible like you and some of my friends do." How many times had I heard that one?

"Well, which book do you not understand?"

"Leviticus."

"Leviticus? Well, I don't even understand Leviticus at times!" We both busted out laughing. In the South we bust, not burst!

She was precious and so honest with me. I gave her the Read the Bible Through in a Year plan and asked this question, "Now, when can you get started, before the baby's first feed or after?"

She sat there a few minutes as we walked through her day. She heard herself admit that she spent well over an hour on Facebook and even more time on the phone with her mom and family. Her face lit up and she said, "I should have my Bible study before those things, shouldn't I?"

With a smile I responded, "Oh yes, you should! And you know what? God will direct you and bless you for putting Him first before others each day. You need to connect with your community of friends on Facebook, but not before Him. You should continue to touch base with Mom, but maybe not as often? Think it over, and trust God to tell you, but be ready, He will talk to you through His Word."

Before the week had ended, she called me and with excitement exclaimed, "Mrs. Loyd, you'll never believe what God has shown me these last few days!"

I said, "Oh yes I would, dear girl. Oh yes, I would!"

Oh me, the things we get twisted about! Pick up a yearly plan or ask me for one and I will send it to you. Most Bibles include a yearly guide of reading God's Word. And remember that this is just a guide. No one is dictating to you how many chapters you must read, because, dear friend, this is between you and God as you get to know Him just a little bit better today than you did yesterday. Mark off the chapter(s) as you read, and eventually you will have read every Word God has written just for you!

Until next time, Lord willing,

Sharon

HOW SWEET IT IS!

The heavens declare the glory of God; and the firmament sheweth his handywork. Day unto day uttereth speech, and night unto night sheweth knowledge. There is no speech nor language, where their voice is not heard. Their line is gone out through all the earth, and their words to the end of the world. In them hath he set a tabernacle for the sun, Which is as a bridegroom coming out of his chamber, and rejoiceth as a strong man to run a race. His going forth is from the end of the heaven, and his circuit unto the ends of it: and there is nothing hid from the heat thereof. The law of the LORD is perfect, converting the soul: the testimony of the LORD is sure, making wise the simple. The statutes of the LORD are right, rejoicing the heart: the commandment of the LORD is pure, enlightening the eyes. The fear of the LORD is clean, enduring for ever: the judgments of the LORD are true and righteous altogether. More to be desired are they than gold, yea, than much fine gold: sweeter also than honey and the honeycomb. Moreover by them is thy servant warned: and in keeping of them there is great reward. Who can understand his errors? cleanse thou me from secret faults. Keep back thy servant also from presumptuous sins; let them not have dominion over me:

then shall I be upright, and I shall be innocent from the great transgression. Let the words of my mouth, and the meditation of my heart, be acceptable in thy sight, O LORD, my strength, and my redeemer. (Psalm 19:1–14)

I am a pretty simple person. I am not what you would call a "brain," and I have always had to work hard for a passing grade in school. Knowledge only came easy to me in one subject, gym. I loved that forty-five-minute stretch of time when I could finally excel in something at school. There wasn't a sport or game that I would shy away from and give my all to win. Whether it was kickball, volleyball, softball, basketball, doing the most sit-ups, or hanging from the bar the longest, I wanted to come in first. Even in our Awana program, I was the worst at Bible memorization, but the best at the Olympics. My parents had boxes full of trophies, medals, and certificates I had won over the years, from catching the biggest fish to the President's Award for physical fitness. If there was a physical competition, you could bet your bottom dollar I was involved and loved it.

Mom and Dad always warned me that one day sports wouldn't be important anymore. I didn't believe them, and I thought they were old fuddy-duddies who had lost their minds. I went off to college and again struggled to pass bonehead English, but my volleyball team was the best. I just couldn't make the leap from play to study. It didn't interest me at all; I liked physical strength, not mental, until one day I got an English teacher who gave me an assignment that changed everything. She wanted me to write a descriptive paragraph. I was introduced to a new and wonderful best friend: words. Mom and Dad were right—sports were no longer important. Go figure.

I wore my library card out as I began delving into how people put words together and crafted a story for me to enjoy. I would read something from every genre, and even if the book bored me, I wanted to know how it would end, so I would read away. Along about the same time, I was challenged about my walk with God and reading the Book of all books, the Bible. Early in the morning, I would make my way out by the lake and read and talk to God. I love thinking back on those times watching the Canadian geese glide across the water and the way the sun would come out and greet me as if I was the only person in the world for whom its rays were shining.

I have watched that same sun rise in its brilliance over the Adriatic Sea, set in flaming color on the Amazon River, and play peekaboo through the clouds above the Alps. I have stared longingly at the moon while lying in a hammock in the middle of the jungle and hunted constellations in the middle of the Caribbean. I have studied the art of Michelangelo in the Sistine Chapel, the smile of da Vinci's Mona Lisa at the Louvre in Paris, and stained-glass windows in the old stately churches of England. I have hiked up waterfalls and fished for piranha in hidden lakes while monkeys played in the trees above and pink dolphins swam around me. I have watched rare birds high up in the mountains, called crocodiles from their hiding places, bungee jumped from great heights, and toured the canals of Venice in a gondola. All of these marvelous things I have been blessed to see and do in my life have made me appreciate the world that my God created and the way He announces Himself no matter what the language, culture, or time of day or night. My God proclaims Himself to be the most mighty and wonderful of all as He rages in a hurricane or delicately opens the petals of a lily. Nature tells us where His footsteps have softly fallen through time, and it truly is magnificent. But none of it compares to the moments when I open the old black Book and read God's Words written as if just for me. It never bores me, and even though I know what is going to happen at the end, I still read it over and over again as if for the very first time.

David was establishing the very same thoughts in Psalm 19. Here is a man who had observed life in the sheep pastures and welcomed the dewy morning, knowing his flock had made it safely through the night. He had heard the thud of Goliath's body when it hit the ground and tasted victory all because of five little rocks he picked from a stream in faith that God would prevail. He had watched the sun set while hiding from Saul in the mouths of caves and listening to the water drops echoing in hollowness of something formed by the finger of God. I think he watched and listened and took note of everything around him that showed him God was real and powerful, and after telling us how wonderful his life and experiences were, it paled at the doctrine of God's words. He saw the perfection of what God was teaching him and how beautiful holiness really was. It was sweeter than the honey he was going to eat later that day. It is almost as if he is reaching through time encouraging us to read, really read, and feast on God's Word. And just think: he only had heard and read a small portion of what you and I have today.

Look, Mom has given us a practical plan for our Bible reading and walk with God, so let's do it. And David has told us about what God's Word will do for us, so let's put it to the test. I believe we will find that it will bring us back to God when we wander off the path. It will show us the difference between folly and wisdom. It will make our hearts rejoice. It will lead us in the way we ought to be going. And it will teach us right from wrong. We don't need to look any further or add to it. God's Word is perfect. That means it is whole, entire, and all that we need. It is the very best way to really get to know Him better.

If I could never write another word, I would end here telling you how sweet God's Word is and how much I believe we should read it.

Until next time, Lord willing,

Sheri

AMAZING GRACE

"But unto every one of us is given grace according to the measure of the gift of Christ" (Ephesians 4:7).

A young child was sent to my office for biting another child. When this happens, we call the biting child's parents *and* the parents of the bitten child. (Sounds like a good name for a movie!) This little girl knew she was wrong but kept drawing attention to the fact that another child had first kicked her. I allowed the little one time to cry and watched her literally spit out her version of what happened. But the fact remained: she bit another person.

"I want my mommy," she wailed. I wailed back that we both had to be at school that day.

She cried some more, peeking over her tears to see if she was getting through to me. She wasn't!

I knew she would eventually surrender, wanting to join her classmates for recess, so I decided that this time out wouldn't last that long. I was right and she went back to class, but not until I called her mom and spoke to her in front of the child. She wailed more loudly during this time, but the mom knew her child and said, "Tell her I will take care of it when I get there." After a short scream and lamentations of sort, she quickly joined her friends.

At the end of school, the mom came, and the little one saw me and said, "My mommy came to pick me up!" Then she grabbed her mom's hand, jumped up and down in delight, and began pulling her mom's arm to their car. I watched them walk away as tears literally came to my eyes. Oh how much we need someone to be "for us" when we make fatuous, quick decisions that could devastate us and others. I wish my blunders were as simple as this little one's, don't you?

Before you and I were born again, we made mistakes that may shadow us the rest of our lives, and, yes, Christ has forgiven us, but the fact remains there may be some heavy consequences that follow. A good bite leaves a mark, or did you know that? So as you join this trip to knowing God, you will find the road to be quite narrow the longer you travel. But, dear friend, God is "for you!" He tells us in 2 Corinthians 12:9, "And he said unto me, My grace is sufficient for thee: for my strength is made perfect in weakness. Most gladly therefore will I rather glory in my infirmities, that the power of Christ may rest upon me." Do you understand that God loves us no matter how rotten we were before we received this grace of His? I don't understand His grace like I should, but I'm learning that this saving grace is His to give to *us* first at salvation, but then, my friend, He offers us serving grace! Just recently some of my favorite preachers have talked about this serving grace, and it is becoming more and more real to me.

Praise God for saving grace. "For by grace are ye saved through faith; and that not of yourselves: it is the gift of God: Not of works, lest any man should boast" (Ephesians 2:8–9). Our faith actively receives this belief while God bestows more grace. No works are involved in saving grace. It is His to give! We reach out and receive it. There are no works involved and neither baptism. It is Him *alone!*

The first time I was baptized, I was dunked three times forward. Our pastor baptized me in the name of the Father, dunk, in the name of the Son, dunk, and in the name of the Holy Spirit, final dunk! None of those dunkings saved me, and neither did joining the church save me. Those two obedient acts were very important to my growth but not to salvation. Jesus's blood on the cross was shed for my rotten, stinking self and for the whole world for those who believe. His Grace is the unmerited eternal salvation of God. It is the opposite of what you and I deserve, friend. Do you have this saving grace, or are you wandering out there, trying to figure out how to make the detours work for you. If you and I are ever going to experience God's serving grace, we must relinquish our way and surrender to His Way!

> "And I thank Christ Jesus our Lord, who hath enabled me, for that he counted me faithful, putting me into the ministry; Who was before a blasphemer, and a persecutor, and injurious: but I obtained mercy, because I did it ignorantly in unbelief. And the grace of our Lord was exceeding abundant with faith and love which is in Christ Jesus" (1 Timothy 1:12–14).

Until next time, Lord willing,

Sharon

WHAT SEEK YE?

"And the two disciples heard him speak, and they followed
Jesus. Then Jesus turned, and saw them following, and
saith unto them, What seek ye? They said unto him,
Rabbi, (which is to say, being interpreted, Master,) where
dwellest thou? He saith unto them, Come and see. They
came and saw where he dwelt, and abode with him that
day: for it was about the tenth hour" (John 1:37–39).

I remember one time, as a young college student, I was walking
down a hallway and saw the man who had just preached in
chapel. His sermon had been very profound, so I trailed him until
I caught up and said, "Brother So-and-So, I sure enjoyed your
preaching today." He immediately turned, towering over me, and
demanded to know what it was specifically that I enjoyed. His
abruptness scared me and took me off guard to the point that I
forgot who I was and what I was doing, and I froze. Seriously, my
mind went so blank that I couldn't even remember what he had
preached on! Then I remembered an illustration I thought he had
used, and I hurriedly repeated it and told him how good it was.
His eyes seemed to stare straight into my soul with their withering
glance, and he promptly turned on his heel and walked away. It
was at this moment my wits returned from their vacation, and I
remembered that he wasn't the one who had told that illustration.
Rather, it had come from *yesterday's* chapel sermon by a completely

different preacher. Talk about embarrassing! My cheeks went hot, and I felt miserable. I never spoke to that man directly again for fear of what he might say to me. I avoided him at all cost for the rest of my years at school, and truth be told, if I saw him today, I wouldn't relish the thought of having to speak to him.

Andrew and John were John the Baptist's disciples. They had just heard their own chapel sermon where John declared that Jesus was the Lamb of God. Imagine how thrilled they must have been! As Jesus began making His way away from the area, Andrew and John followed Him. And that's when Jesus turned and questioned them, "What seek ye?" Can you fathom what you would do if you were physically there that day and Jesus turned and looked at you and began questioning you? I don't know whether they hesitated or not, but they ask Jesus where he lived. Jesus knew they wanted to get to know Him better and didn't make fun of their asking where he dwelled. He told them to "come and see." It must have been an exciting moment for the two men as they accepted Jesus's invitation to follow Him. Unlike me that day at college with the chapel speaker, they didn't hide from Jesus or decline the invitation and avoid Jesus. No, they followed Him.

I have to say, I am not a great Christian. I don't excel in my faith as I should. I don't consider myself a great prayer warrior or even a mediocre one. I struggle with my flesh and battle quite frequently in my spiritual life. And you know what I have come to realize? So does everyone else. We all feel like we can't get to know the Lord as well as the next guy. We think preachers have some special inroad with the Lord that we don't have, and we often feel inadequate to teach a Sunday school or ladies' Bible study. Don't get me wrong. We can find thrilling heights of peace and joy when we are sitting alone in our homes reading His Word while sipping on a cup of coffee or tea. We bask in His presence and find it to be an amazing time, until we go to church or work. Then we begin comparing ourselves among ourselves. Someone looks at us sideways or makes an offhand comment that leaves us hurt or angry. Our children are disobedient, and we argue with our husbands. The week wears on, and our prayers don't seem to be getting answered, and we assume it must be because we are insignificant little dots in the vast array of Christians God has to hear from each day. Long forgotten are those precious moments alone with Christ and His Word. We begin to shrivel as we doubt, and then all of a sudden, He speaks to us through a scripture, as if to say, "What seek ye?" Let's not seize up and blurt out what we think He wants to hear or repeat something we have heard another say in a prayer! When we are invited to fellowship with Him at our prayer spot, let's not lose our minds and babble vain repetitions! Why waste His time or ours? Let's just be honest with Him. If our minds are prone to wander, then tell Him, "Lord, my mind wants to wander off to think about the laundry or my teaching schedule today, so would you help my weakness? Would you guide my thoughts and protect my mind with the helmet of salvation? Lord, I don't feel like I belong here at your feet or even in your presence, but I know you promise that you will draw nigh unto me if I draw nigh unto you, so here I am, just as I am."

Don't turn tail and run when God's Holy Spirit draws your attention to a verse. Don't wander off, thinking He doesn't really want to spend time with you. You are of no less importance than the next Christian! You are allowed to come to Him. You are wanted in His presence. You matter.

The next time God nudges your heart, don't lose your mind like I did with that chapel speaker. Follow His lead into His presence and dwell there with Him. Prepare yourself to withstand the day ahead and all that awaits you. He sees what is coming, and He wants to equip you with what you need. Why would He do that for someone if He didn't care about them? He cares about you and your life.

> "If any man serve me, let him follow me; and where I am, there shall also my servant be: if any man serve me, him will my Father honour" (John 12:26).

Until next time, Lord willing,

Sheri

IT'S ALL BECAUSE OF GOD'S AMAZING GRACE

"But by the grace of God I am what I am: and his grace which was bestowed upon me was not in vain; but I laboured more abundantly than they all: yet not I, but the grace of God which was with me" (1 Corinthians 15:10).

For the life of me, I don't know why it took me so long to understand a little bit better this matter concerning God's grace. Maybe you are like me and have totally gotten the concept of saving grace, but for years you have seen yourself not capable of doing much for the Lord Jesus Christ whether in the ministry of the local church or just sharing the Gospel. Have you felt inadequate, not worthy, or just plain scared, or all of these? You are not alone. In order to know God better, and this is what we are trying to do on this journey, we have to look at this matter of His grace as we serve God. We can't do it by ourselves, or it becomes about us and not about Him. So how are you doing? Feeling weaker? Jesus can empathize with our weaknesses, because in His humanity, He was faced with those weaknesses, not that He was weak, but He faced it for you and for me. He faced what we face head on. That really makes me feel better, and it should you too, dear friend. He is our strength. The grace that He offers to us in our weakest moment makes us strong enough to overcome any obstacle. Usually, *we* are the obstacle. As we exercise that truth or put it to action, we can do *all* things because it goes and comes through Jesus Christ. Again, remember: Jesus never succumbed to temptation! In my human flesh, I cannot comprehend that, but if we are to ever cross Jordan, so to speak, we have to grab that truth and pack it our purses!

> "Seeing then that we have a great high priest, that is passed into the heavens, Jesus the Son of God, let us hold fast our profession. For we have not an high priest which cannot be touched with the feeling of our infirmities; but was in all points tempted like as we are, yet without sin. Let us therefore come boldly unto the throne of grace, that we may obtain mercy, and find grace to help in time of need" (Hebrews 4:14–16).

So, what is holding you back from ministry? Admit it, say it out loud to God, and go back to the turn of the road to God's dwelling place. Psalms 90 and 91 will be a nice refresher to remember that—this is where it must begin.

The first time I heard John R. Rice I thought, "This poor ole man's eyes are going to slide right off his face, today, while we are sitting here looking at him!" Little did I know about this great man of God with droopy eyes and his lovely wife. I can still hear his weeping voice pleading to all of us to come boldly to God's throne of grace for mercy in our times of need. I am blessed of God to have been a friend to John R. Rice. But did you know that Brother Rice never really felt the call to preach? He just started serving God, and by God's grace, He used him in mighty ways. May I encourage you to read the life of John R. Rice, and if you have read about him, share it with a sister in Christ. Sheri had the privilege of visiting in his home and shared with her dad and me that he and his wife lived very frugally. He was so gifted in writing, singing, and of course, preaching.

> "Whereof I was made a minister, according to the gift of the grace of God given unto me by the effectual working of his power. Unto me, who am less than the least of all saints, is this grace given, that I should preach among the Gentiles the unsearchable riches of Christ; And to make all men see what is the fellowship of the mystery, which from the beginning of the world hath been hid in God, who created all things by Jesus Christ" (Ephesians 3:7–9).

Brother Rice's mom died when he was nine years old, and years later he found out while reading a letter she had written to another relative of theirs that his mom called him "her preacher boy." When he read that, it did something to him, and a seed was planted in his mind to completely sell out to God. May I say, "Don't be fearful of encouraging your children to serve God in ministry and when they ask you, tell them!" I am so thankful for the many young people who have come through our Christian school and gone on to serve God as missionaries, preachers, evangelists, and other ministries. Every young person who has come to me questioning the ministry, I have gladly said, "Just make that first step and God will do the rest." It is called "serving grace," folks, and all of us can receive it as freely as we did His saving grace.

Saul of Tarsus is such a good example of what God can do with a Christian-killing maniac! Read the account in Acts 9 of Saul, who became converted to do the impossible only because of God's amazing, saving, serving grace! Paul and Brother Rice lived this "serving grace" and left us a legacy of truth regarding grace. Everyone hated Paul and couldn't believe he was actually a born-again believer after the news of his consenting to the deaths of many Christians. I would feel the same, wouldn't you? God granted him the grace to not be bitter as he traveled to face the disbelieving Christians. They feared for their lives when Paul was around. Eventually, Paul's reputation was better, and by God's grace, hundreds were saved through the ministry of Paul. My soul, just think how much you and I have grown while reading the epistles of Paul! So maybe you are struggling with the thoughts that you could never sing in the choir, or teach Sunday school like so and so, or drive a bus, or go soul winning. Yep, so did Paul with his thorn in the flesh, but what did God say to him? "My grace is sufficient!"

Until next time, Lord willing,

Sharon

DON'T GET OFF AT
THE WRONG STOP!

Paul, an apostle of Jesus Christ by the commandment of God our Saviour, and Lord Jesus Christ, which is our hope; Unto Timothy, my own son in the faith: Grace, mercy, and peace, from God our Father and Jesus Christ our Lord. As I besought thee to abide still at Ephesus, when I went into Macedonia, that thou mightest charge some that they teach no other doctrine, Neither give heed to fables and endless genealogies, which minister questions, rather than godly edifying which is in faith: so do. Now the end of the commandment is charity out of a pure heart, and of a good conscience, and of faith unfeigned: From which some having swerved have turned aside unto vain jangling; Desiring to be teachers of the law; understanding neither what they say, nor whereof they affirm. (1 Timothy 1:1–7).

My first time in Brooklyn, I was invited to join a group headed to the city by subway. I got my children ready, and we were excited to take our first ride on the famous subways of NYC. We bought our tickets and found a spot to sit in the train car. I was chatting away with a colleague when we came to the first stop. The doors opened and my oldest son, who was only twelve years old at the time, promptly exited the car and stood facing me. He had a kind of puzzled look on his face because we were not getting off with him. I jumped and screamed at the same time, warning him to get back in before the doors closed. He quickly entered as the doors slammed shut. He had narrowly escaped being lost in the middle of a strange city. My heart still races when I think about what could have happened that day. I am glad I was near enough to him and paying attention.

Paul is warning Timothy in I Timothy chapter 1 about not getting off at the wrong station. He doesn't want Timothy to blindly follow the opening doors. He makes it clear that there are those who would teach a hodgepodge of things and produce a whole lot of questions, none of which were edifying. He tells Timothy to focus on the end of the commandment, the destination of his faith—charity, a good conscience, and faith unfeigned.

I have been a Christian for over thirty years. I have been in the ministry full time for over twenty of those years. During that time, trust me, many a person has come along with some fables and vain jangling. Sadly, there have been times when I took heed and got off at the wrong stop. I wasted my time lost in someone else's false interpretation of the scripture, and it aggravates me to no end. I am writing this today to make sure we don't get off on the wrong path in our quest to know God better. He is not found in spooky beliefs and weird, far-out places. No, He is found in truth. His dwelling is grace and truth, not ideas and speculations. Make sure that what you are listening to by way of preaching or teaching measure up to the truth of the Holy Scriptures. God forbid that Mom and I lead you astray! Be a Berean Christian and daily search the scriptures for yourself. Don't be a foolish woman led off by every wind of doctrine that blows the curtains in your house.

Mark and I teach our children to make decisions based on scripture. Not just because we tell them that it is what the Bible says, but for them to search it out and decide. They have not always made the right choices. Sometimes I cringe when I see them about to make the wrong decision. But all four of my children will tell you that they believe God's Word to be their basis, and not man's traditions. You and I need to be constantly aware of where we are on this journey. We don't need to get off on bunny trails that waste our time and our provisions. Let's be reading the scripture on our own, daily. Let us compare His words with His words and stand firmly on truth. God has been merciful to me and given me two pastors during my life who hold firmly to the Word of God. My pastor, as a young person, was Dr. Andy Bloom. He never swerved aside to vain jangling. He always pointed me toward truth in every single sermon. Matter of fact, a sermon I heard from him just recently changed my outlook on a situation and helped me. Why? Because he taught truth. Dr. John Smith became my pastor in 1998. He is a preacher of preachers. He preaches the Word and points our church toward truth. I remember the day in his office when he taught me what the doctrine of imputation is. He quoted scripture to me and opened my eyes to what Jesus had actually done for me at salvation. Truth, not tradition.

As you seek after God and read His Word, don't get off on the wrong stop and get lost. Sometimes these popular new devotionals look inviting and so good, but beneath some of their words is a faulty foundation. If you are ever unsure, ask your husband or preacher to clarify things you don't understand. Keep a commentary nearby so you can study. And ask God to guide you to *all* truth, never fiction.

If you truly want to know Him better, get to know what He says about Himself. You can't err by following God's Word.

Until next time, Lord willing,

Sheri

GOD WANTS TO BE IN
THE DRIVER'S SEAT

For today I want us to look at scripture that explains more of God's grace for serving. I have taken a few (there are so many!) and tried to give a practical way to look at this serving grace. There are many more scriptures, but I am praying that the ones chosen will be enough for you as we journey in grace land, and maybe your mind just went to another Graceland, but trust me: that is *not* where I am going with this.

Don't you just love looking out the window as you drive down a country lane and inhale the beauty of God and His creations? Consider this grace to be a field full of trees loaded with fruit ready for you to pick. We could call it "Grace Territory," if you please. It is yours for the picking!

1. Grace in meeting the needs of God's people

> "Moreover, brethren, we do you to wit of the grace of God bestowed on the churches of Macedonia; How that in a great trial of affliction the abundance of their joy and their deep poverty abounded unto the riches of their liberality" (2 Corinthians 8:1–2).

Our church is called on weekly to supply the needs of people outside the church and many times outside of the faith. God's leaders must be very careful to not abuse the church people and the monies of the church for wrong reasons, but as the need comes, God's people can rally around, seek His face, and then receive the grace to get the job done. It takes wisdom and the Word of God to know how sometimes. Maybe you are really good at sewing, cleaning homes, making crafts, taking care of children, doing laundry, writing letters, fixing meals, or organizing any of these areas. God's people have needs, and you may be able to exercise the grace of God in you to meet that need. Oh, how precious are those people who seek ways to help those in need. A caring and giving spirit brings a smile to our Lord Jesus Christ. Are you one of those persons called on to meet a family's need as simple as taking a meal to that family or helping the family care for a sick child, or are you afraid you just can't do it? Here we go. Ask God for the grace to do what *He* wants you to do! The fruit of that tree will reproduce more than you ever dreamed!

2. Grace to help in time of need in your own personal life or in the personal life of another

> "Let us therefore come boldly unto the throne of grace, that we may obtain mercy, and find grace to help in time of need" (Hebrews 4:16).

My husband and I received three separate calls in the same day from people in our church who had dire needs for their families. We listened; we prayed and asked God to intervene in the lives of these lovely people and their families. Sometimes you may not know what to pray or what to do, but that is when

God steps in and does what you cannot do. Don't beat yourself up if you can't figure it out. You are just like the rest of us. We all have to trust in that wonderful grace of God and obtain mercy to be the instrument of God's help as it flows through us. Then just claim the truth of Hebrews 4:16!

3. Grace is to be received and used—not abused!

> "As every man hath received the gift, even so minister the same one to another, as good stewards of the manifold grace of God. If any man speak, let him speak as the oracles of God; if any man minister, let him do it as of the ability which God giveth: that God in all things may be glorified through Jesus Christ, to whom be praise and dominion for ever and ever. Amen" (1 Peter 4:10–11).

None of us have arrived, friend, and if we do anything worth doing it is only because of God's grace. I've seen people who have been blessed beyond measure, and then slowly, their heads swell with pride, and they begin to feel like they have had something to do with it. Before long these dear people change, and shame rests at their back door. There *will be* a fall if the foundation is not right! It is God's grace, not your ability or my ability!

4. Grace to serve God effectually by teaching and preaching His Word

> "Whereof I was made a minister, according to the gift of the grace of God given unto me by the effectual working of his power. Unto me, who am

less than the least of all saints, is this grace given, that I should preach among the Gentiles the unsearchable riches of Christ" (Ephesians 3:7–8).

"Wherefore we receiving a kingdom which cannot be moved, let us have grace, whereby we may serve God acceptably with reverence and godly fear" (Hebrews 12:28).

Pastor Andy is always asking us to pray for him to have utterance to preach to men as they are. He works diligently at reminding us that it is God's work and God's word. If there is any success in it at all, it is because of God's grace. Is there a need where you are? Are you willing to open the Word and teach another as God's grace is bestowed upon you? How many times have I heard young men say, "I just can't preach! I'm not smart enough, not educated enough and besides, I'm scared to be in front of people." Well, good! You are the perfect candidate. Now give up and let God take over. Don't you just love it when you witness people who you thought would never amount to a hill of beans come back around and are on fire for the Lord! God created us, and He for sure can figure out what to do with us, if we will only realize that it is Him and not us! Put God in the driver's seat, move over, and enjoy the ride, for heaven's sake.

Now, what are you waiting for?

Until next time, Lord willing

Sharon

HE IS FAITHFUL

As we take this journey together getting to know our Lord better, I felt it appropriate to share one of my favorite traits of this awesome, wonderful God! He is faithful! So now let's open our eyes wide and take a long look at just how wonderful our Creator, our Father, really is. Be encouraged by what you are about to read, because this is the one to whom you pray, the one you lean on, and the one you praise. And, even more amazingly, He is the one hearing and answering your prayers, holding you up, and receiving your praise, of which He is worthy.

1. Our God is faithful.

> "But the Lord is faithful, who shall stablish you, and keep you from evil" (2 Thessalonians 3:3).

Listen, I don't know where you are in your life today. I don't know if this has been one terrible week or month (or year). Maybe you are just tired and worn out. Maybe today has dawned heavy on you—like an anvil on your head. Or perhaps you have seen some great victories lately and are full of peace. Whatever the case may be and wherever we find ourselves, let's promise to be honest. Let's not look at all the junk surrounding us or the problems waiting on us at work. Let's not look down our noses from the mountaintop at those still in the valley. Rather, let's open our eyes and take a good long look at God. See Him for who He really is. He is faithful.

He brought you through the last time, didn't He? He comforted you in that moment when no one else knew you were crumpled and crying in the shower, didn't He? He paid that bill, healed that wound, brought you up, set your feet on solid ground, and blessed you, didn't He? Remember? Remember His presence? Just because you may have forgotten doesn't mean He has. Because He is faithful. He is faithful every single day, every single second, and He cannot break His promises.

> "If we believe not, yet he abideth faithful: he cannot deny himself" (2 Timothy 2:13).

2. He promised you a way of escape. Look around. It is there.

> "There hath no temptation taken you but such as is common to man: but God is faithful, who will not suffer you to be tempted above that ye are able; but will with the temptation also make a way to escape, that ye may be able to bear it" (1 Corinthians 10:13).

If you are contemplating turning your direction down a path the faithful God has *not* led you, stop! He wants you to make the decision to turn toward Him. Jesus told Peter in the garden to pray, but Peter slept and then denied Christ. Make the decision to pray about what you are about to do. And if you are headed where you shouldn't, turn around and run in the right direction before you make a mess of things. God is faithfully standing there, offering you the *right* option.

3. He is controlling the situation. Relax in Him.

> "Wherefore let them that suffer according to the will of God commit the keeping of their souls to him in well doing, as unto a faithful Creator" (1 Peter 4:19).

Do you remember when Jesus stood before Pilate? He knew He was the faithful God. He knew He had created every single soul before Him who mocked Him, gnashed their teeth at Him, yelled profanities at Him, but Jesus was faithful in His suffering, because He had a promise to keep, a promise made to those priests screaming, "Crucify Him!" and a promise to you and me. He *had* to suffer in order to do His own will! If He has placed you in a position that seems unbearable, offer to stay there as long as He needs you to. Easy for me to say? No, not hardly. But it's something I have prayed, something I have watched my mom pray and my dad and sister live. And every time, through every seemingly unbearable situation, God showed Himself faithful. If you are there, then know for a fact that God's will is performing something far greater than you can imagine and you can relax in Him.

4. He will *not* leave you alone. Don't quit. He won't.

> "Faithful is he that calleth you, who also will do it" (1 Thessalonians 5:24).

Don't quit. Don't quit. Don't quit. Try one more day. Find someone to pray with you and remind yourself of all the times God was faithful in your life. Keep going. You are *not* alone. God faithfully remains loyal to His promises. He will do it! Let Him.

5.   He *will* Forgive you. He *will* cleanse you.

> "If we confess our sins, he is faithful and just to forgive us our sins, and to cleanse us from all unrighteousness" (1 John 1:9).

Don't be prisoner to your past sins for one more second. Confess up. God is faithful and will cleanse you. Walk away clean and don't go wallowing around in the past again.

It feels easy to throw our hands up and say, "Forget it!" It may keep us tightly cocooned in our nest of betrayal or in fear of being hurt again. But it will stop us from getting to know Him better. Just think back on all that you have been through, each time you threw the towel in and let the pieces fall where they would. Did God ever leave you in your confusion? Nope. He wooed you back and ministered to your hurts. He was there, because He is faithful. Why not take Him at His word? Let Him do what he needs to do in your life right now and trust Him.

Until next time, Lord willing,

Sheri

SOMEBODY, PLEASE

"Sow to yourselves in righteousness, reap in mercy; break up your fallow ground: for it is time to seek the LORD, till he come and rain righteousness upon you. Ye have plowed wickedness, ye have reaped iniquity; ye have eaten the fruit of lies: because thou didst trust in thy way, in the multitude of thy mighty men" (Hosea 10:12–13).

"According to their pasture, so were they filled; they were filled, and their heart was exalted; therefore have they forgotten me" (Hosea 13:6).

"O Israel, thou hast destroyed thyself; but in me is thine help" (Hosea 13:9).

"Therefore turn thou to thy God: keep mercy and judgment, and wait on thy God continually" (Hosea 12:6).

I suppose the darkest days of my life will be remembered for as long as I live. As a seven-year-old young girl cuddling my six-year-old sister, I literally watched the stars in the dark, summer night while listening to drunken men and women laugh and slobber all over each other. The liquor store's blinking, enticing light caught our attention, but we ran for shelter toward an old, dilapidated barn. The climb inside the barn seemed an eternity while my sister cried with such intense weeping. I thought we would die, but with trembling, small fingers we made it up the ladder and quickly shoved ourselves into a corner.

Mama had left us for the last time, and Daddy could not be found. He had no idea what this night held for us and certainly did not know that Mama had walked off and left everything— *everything!* Oh, how my Daddy loved my Mama! My sister cried most of the night, but somewhere in the wee hours of the morning she hushed and drifted off into sleep. The agony that children feel and experience because of the sins of their moms and dads do so much damage, a damage that sometimes is never repaired—until somebody helps them, loves them, and shows them the love of Christ!

Sometimes your journey through the Word of God will bring up a memory like this one has for me. Hosea is very close to my heart. Every year when I read it, I learn something from it that I did not get the previous year, but every time I read it, I am reminded of the sin of my mama. Maybe as you read God's Word you are like me. A memory pops up, and you may think, "I dealt with that, Lord, a long time ago," and probably you did, but sometimes maybe you didn't. It's very important on this journey to be honest with God and talk it through with Him. He already knows your heart anyway, so just be honest. It is impossible to know Him more, if we are not straightforward with Him.

The nation of Israel left God. They walked away from everything— everything good, decent, and truthful—to follow their idolatrous ways. They wanted their own way and not God's way.

> "My people are destroyed for lack of knowledge: because thou hast rejected knowledge, I will also reject thee, that thou shalt be no priest to me: seeing thou hast forgotten

the law of thy God, I will also forget thy children"
(Hosea 4:6).

Hosea is a difficult book to comprehend in one sense, and yet it
makes all the sense in the world! We don't like to ponder these
thoughts of a harlot, adultery, and rebellion, because we had
rather hear about love, faith, and righteousness. My God taught
me a lesson in life long before I knew Jesus as my Savior. Go
figure! Somewhere in that darkest night, I cried out to God,
"Somebody, somebody please help me!"

The broken glass beneath my feet began to pierce deeply, but
nothing compared to the fear in my little heart that night. I knew
that my sister and I would be the victims of a terrible abuse if
someone didn't rescue us. That someone was God Himself! I can't
explain it, folks, but that night He placed a shield of protection
where no man or woman would dare enter. Just the mere cry from
a child's heart or even a man or woman in another country who
doesn't know about Jesus's saving grace can capture the ear of an
awesome, wonderful God. He will send help! I knew God heard
me. He was all that I had! I shall never, never forget that night.

> "For their mother hath played the harlot: she that
> conceived them hath done shamefully: for she said, I
> will go after my lovers, that give me my bread and my
> water, my wool and my flax, mine oil and my drink"
> (Hosea 2:5).

Now you may judge me for telling such a thing that has brought
shame to our family, and you may even ask, "Why would you tell
something like this about yourself?" Do you know why? I want
you to see how the scriptures teach us about Him *and* about us, as
sorry and lowly as we are sometimes. God has given us *everything*,
and we walk away from it, wipe our lips, and say, "I haven't done

so badly." I am no different than my mama, and neither are you, because the Bible says that we are all sinners!

Every Word of God must be read—every Word, over and over and over, year after year after year. You and I will always grow as long as we don't put the Book down and walk away from *everything* that is beautiful, just for us! He waits. He listens for you to get up, get your coffee or tea, and go to Him. He watches you read Him and loves on you, but He also warns you of the dark side of sin that will destroy this sweet fellowship. Thank God He cares enough to be honest with us.

"I will heal their backsliding, I will love them freely: for mine anger is turned away from him" (Hosea 14:4).

If His anger turned away, then so should we do the same. Maybe for you it is time to make that call to someone who has hurt you and make amends and turn back to *everything*! My parents eventually became born-again believers. They would be the first to admit their sins and mistakes with their children. For years we were separated from Mama, but she began to look us up, one by one, and make amends. She was a saved woman and now lives with her Savior. My Daddy became a Christian after a massive heart attack. He was one blessed man! He died of another heart attack at the age of fifty-eight. He was too young to die, and he knew his body was in trouble years before he went on to heaven to join his Savior. I am blessed to see both of my parents saved and now, living with Jesus!

Until next time, Lord willing,

Sharon

TRUST GOD WITH THE PAIN

"And Joseph said unto them, Fear not: for am I in the place of God? But as for you, ye thought evil against me; but God meant it unto good, to bring to pass, as it is this day, to save much people alive" (Genesis 50:19–20).

As a child I was a little on the naughty side. I was into everything. If something made a noise, I wanted to know why. If there were drawers I had never opened, I wanted to find out what was inside. Mama often reprimanded me for snooping, but in my mind, I was exploring the wide, wide world. Well, one day, I got curious about where the ants went, so I followed a trail of them to their hill and shoved all the mound away that they had worked so hard to build, and I discovered the hole leading into the ground. I grabbed a nearby stick and began to dig. I was so intent on all the digging I didn't notice the ants had gotten mad and declared war on me, until my arms and legs began to burn with the bites of a hundred angry ants. I ran to the spigot and washed my little arms and legs off, but man, those welts hurt for hours. I think all the ants told their relatives, because ever since, they have exacted their revenge on me for destroying their home. They even must have spoken Portuguese, because the ants down here in Brazil have been no kinder!

You know, sometimes we don't mean to get into trouble, do we? Yet we can be right smack dab in the middle of it, because we aren't being careful. After I dug that ant hole as I child, I never attempted it again, because I knew the pain it could cause me. I can still imagine those angry, red welts on my arms if I think about it long enough. And after you and I get in the middle of a mess in our lives, we don't ever want to go back there again, because that heart pain is often more agonizing than physical pain. You would think that we would steer clear of things that could entangle us into the mistakes of our past at all cost. It's just plain common sense, right? But what about when someone else puts us into the mess and the painful situation is out of our control? What do we do then?

God gave us a wonderful example in the last few chapters of Genesis of how to handle unforeseen and unwarranted problems. Joseph was ripped away from his family, suffered unimaginably at the hands of strangers, and his entire life was altered because of someone else. In the end, however, he had learned a lesson in grace and in faith that was worth every miserable night of weeping he had spent. He shows us how to be Christ-like in our behavior and look at life's trials through the eyes of faith that God is in control.

Joseph showed grace when he forgave his brothers. He showed faith when he told them that God had meant it all for good. Do you think God put this true story in the Bible for us just so we could teach it to children in Sunday school? Of course not! He knew (duh) that we would all need an example to follow. Look, don't treat the Bible (or God for that matter) like a foreign object in your life. The Bible is alive and relevant to me, you, and any other person who wants to read It. The heartache and victories of Joseph have many levels of application, and there is a simple one that you and I can grab hold of today: We can choose grace and faith.

Just this weekend I had to make a choice. Someone used words against one of my children that cut my heart so thoroughly that at the moment I read them, I immediately began crying. I sucked in my breath as I reread what she had written, and I wept. My first reaction was violence. Man, I wanted to get on a plane and fly to where she lives and pummel her with my two fists until I felt like she understood how rotten I thought her words really were. (I know—my flesh can be pretty mean, but I am bringing this down to where we all live on a day-to-day basis. This stuff happens to all of us.) Well, after getting my tears out, going to my husband and talking it over with him, I walked outside and looked up. I stared into the clouds and poured my heart out to the Creator of those clouds and told Him just what I felt about the whole situation. And there before me, I had a choice: grace and faith, or unforgiveness, revenge, and bitterness.

Joseph was a man with the same feelings you and I have today. He had to make a choice to either forgive or not to forgive. He had a choice to have faith in God's sovereign will or take it all into his own human hands. He chose by his own free will to do the right thing. And you and I can too.

After I talked to God, I made a decision. I decided that I would simply let it go. I decided that I would take a step in my spiritual life and learn how to take the high road. I already know the pain that awaits if I were to seek revenge. Lord knows I have done that a *lot* in my life. So why should I seek to entangle myself back into that pain again? That person that spoke against my child meant it for evil, but God used it to let me grow closer to Him. He knew it was all going to happen. He was not shocked. He knew how it would make my husband and me feel, but He wanted it to happen because He wants *me*, little old curious, mean-spirited, rotten Sheri, to draw closer to Him. And you know what? That makes me thank Him for it. I want to get to know Him better!

Is there a choice staring you in the face today? May I encourage you, from one sinner to another, to choose grace and faith? It will be a step closer to knowing God better and you will find some peace there. I know it is hard, and a lot of words like "unfair" and "unjust" are running through your mind, but God is working something in your life, trust Him with the pain. Because in His other hand is the balm of Gilead!

Until next time, Lord willing,

Sheri

DON'T QUIT—JUST KEEP MAKING GOOD BISCUITS!

Simon Peter, a servant and an apostle of Jesus Christ, to them that have obtained like precious faith with us through the righteousness of God and our Savior Jesus Christ: Grace and peace be multiplied unto you through the knowledge of God, and of Jesus our Lord, According as his divine power hath given unto us all things that pertain unto life and godliness, through the knowledge of him that hath called us to glory and virtue: Whereby are given unto us exceeding great and precious promises: that by these ye might be partakers of the divine nature, having escaped the corruption that is in the world through lust. And beside this, giving all diligence, add to your faith virtue; and to virtue knowledge. (2 Peter 1:1–5)

I don't remember the first time Mama helped me make biscuits, but I do remember how delicious the homemade bread was even if she did most of the work. Before Daddy divorced my mom, she would make biscuits every day, and sometimes twice a day, depending on how many workers came from the field for dinner (our lunch was called "dinner" back then). In the mornings, all five of us girls sat at a round table, our chins barely touching the edge of the checkered tablecloth. On the table sat hot grits—smoking grits, we called it—with fresh fried pork and eggs that were gathered that morning, and of course, Mama's biscuits. Mama was a good cook. She just didn't know how to keep all of us and the farm together. She loved us but somewhere she just stopped making biscuits. I look back now as a grandmother and understand her loneliness, her desire to know "stuff" beyond the farm. Her knowledge of God was limited, and she resisted any attempt to go with us to church. That in itself was a dangerous sign that something wasn't quite right. It's risky for a woman to stop doing what she does best in the family because allurements of the world outside can cause havoc to the entire family.

I admit that I struggle with certain words and *knowledge* in this passage is one of them, not because I don't understand its meaning, but because it is such a complicated word for the Christian. Just because we have knowledge of God doesn't mean we *know* Him. Peter must have thought that knowledge was indeed so very important as he used it seven times in 2 Peter, and *every* time he used it, he referred to Christ. There cannot be true knowledge of God without Jesus Christ in us. I really don't want to equat making biscuits to learning about knowledge, but I do want for you and me to see that each ingredient is a "must" as we study these seven attributes in 2 Peter 1. They are necessary for us to move our faith to moving mountains in our lives! Don't you just want to see mountains moved for people and for yourself? The road ahead looks totally impossible for the unbelieving and to the believer *unless* the right ingredients are added but mixed with one another. I don't want to confuse you, so stay with me for this ride. Rest stops are ahead.

In my Bible are these words printed right above 2 Peter 1:3, "Growth in Christ." Growth, isn't that what we desire on this road trip to knowing God? Peter is talking to believers like you and me. God has given us promises to participate in God's divine nature. Why? So we will not fall prey to the corruption that is all around us. Promises are found in God's Word as we study it day in and day out, same place, same time, same Bible. Yes, we may pick up one of the popular authors and read the alphabetized list of promises, *or* we can claim them as we read through God's Word for ourselves. God desires to sit down with us as we listen to Him, and eventually, a promise of truth jumps out and if you are like me, you just sit there in awe! From Genesis to Revelation we have some thirty-eight hundred promises. To me, that is exciting!

> "Whereby are given unto us exceeding great and precious promises: that by these ye might be partakers of the divine nature, having escaped the corruption that is in the world through lust. And beside this, giving all diligence, add to your faith virtue; and to virtue knowledge" (2 Peter 1:4–5).

So we look at the divine nature of God in us and are now ready to exercise our diligence if we have any handy. Check out your diligence, 'cause you will need your steady Eddie, constant zeal, wholeheartedness—your diligence—to add that cup of virtue! Virtue is defined in *The New Defenders's Study Bible* as "spiritual valor, or strength of character." I want to encourage you to take your faith, however little or strong it is, and exhibit this virtue of yours, and if you are weak in valor or strength of character, then tell God! Don't quit on me. Stay for a while until you are able to grab 2 Peter 2: 1–8 *if* you want more perfect vision of who this *awesome, great, loving God* truly is!

Until next time, Lord willing.

Sharon

IS YOUR DRYER SQUEALING?

There is one piece of machinery in my house that I wear out yearly, and that's my clothes dryer. The ones here in Brazil are not built to withstand what I throw into mine. If it is sunny outside, I hang my clothes on the lines, but I live in the mountains where winters are cold and wet. Right now it is summertime here in the southern hemisphere, and we have had a lot of rain and overcast days. My clothes will hang for three days and never dry. Here recently, every time I put a load into the dryer and turned it on, it would begin to squeal. At first, it was just a small squeal and after a few minutes would disappear. But over time, the noise became louder. I tried to ignore it, but the pitch became so irritating that no one could stand it. My daddy didn't raise no dummy, so I got my toolbox out and took the dryer apart to see if I could fix it, but in the end, it proved to be more than I could handle. I had to send it to the repair shop. They told me I had worn out a pulley, a belt, and a bunch of other little things. It cost me three hundred and fifty bucks, and, folks, honestly and simply said as a missionary, I ain't got no money! If I had taken the dryer in when it first started squealing, I could have saved myself a lot of money. But I chose to "try and make do" instead of acknowledging what needed to be done.

Just recently I read John 19–21. I don't know about you, but I can't read that passage of scripture without tears. The account

John gives of Mary Magdalene's moment in the garden with Jesus is remarkable. I love the way Jesus speaks her name but even more so that she recognizes Him.

All of us have a testimony of how God has saved us or brought us out of a difficult situation. We know how it feels when His presence fills our hearts and He fellowships with us personally. Many words in the old hymns have been used to describe that sense of peace and communion, but there really isn't an adequate adjective to describe it, is there? Can you think on a moment right now when you had that sweet fellowship? When you lingered at your prayer time and had to stop for more Kleenex while you read the Word? A hymn stayed on your lips throughout the day and you felt as though your heart was lighter than a feather?

What happens between those perfect days and the ones we normally have? Where is it that we go from Mary Magdalene in the garden to being a doubting Thomas, a betraying Peter, or a quitting Demas? Something has gotten out of whack somewhere along the way, like the squeal of my dryer was telling me something was wrong and needed to be fixed.

I believe it is an everyday struggle. I don't believe for a second that one Christian has more at his or her disposal for his or her walk with God than the next. I believe we all have the entire Word, and we all can walk with and know God. Otherwise, you would have to conclude that God changes from one Christian to the next, and we know that would be a lie! He doesn't change. We do. We let the sin in this world and the consequences of that sin speak louder than His proper Word does. We allow some new theologian to falsely parse the scripture and cause us to doubt what we *already* know to be true. We go through a trial and decide it all isn't worth it, and we lay down our swords and quit.

So, what can we do about it? Take it one day at a time. Let's deal with it today. Right now. Nothing stands between you and a right relationship with God but *you*. I don't care if you are behind prison bars, sitting in the divorce court, nursing a newborn, waiting on your chemo to be over, or heading to the funeral home today to make plans, you *can* immediately be 100 percent right with God. You just have to come to terms with your sin or doubt and acknowledge it to God. Here is a hint: He already knows.

Jesus knew who Mary was seeking that day in the garden. He knew why she wept. But He asked her about it because He wanted her to acknowledge it.

> "Jesus saith unto her, Woman, why weepest thou? whom seekest thou? She, supposing him to be the gardener, saith unto him, Sir, if thou have borne him hence, tell me where thou hast laid him, and I will take him away. Jesus saith unto her, Mary. She turned herself, and saith unto him, Rabboni; which is to say, Master" (John 20:15–16).

God wants us to get to know Him. He doesn't hold Himself back and play hide-and-go-seek with us. He is available and wants us to heed His Words and fellowship with Him. No, every day won't be a peaceful beautiful walk on the outside, but it can be on the inside, and that is what we should strive for!

I know life isn't fair. I know things get us down and hurt us beyond what we think we are capable of handling. But God knows it too! He wants to go through it all *with* you! He isn't against you unless you are living in wickedness. His ears are open to your prayers as long as you aren't making vain repetitions and lying to Him. So why not just stop and pray. Pray right where you are right now. Tell God your sins, repent of it all, and ask

Him to restore that sweet fellowship to you. He will because He cannot break His promises to us.

> "He that covereth his sins shall not prosper: but whoso confesseth and forsaketh them shall have mercy" (Proverbs 28:13).

Tomorrow you will need to take inventory of your life yet again. If you mess up somewhere along the way today, you will need to tell God about it. Seek what He says to do about it and do it. Maintain that fellowship. And don't think for a minute that I am not writing to myself and expressing to my own heart what Sheri needs to do. I am on this earth with you. I battle the world and its call every day. I get spiritually lazy on the mission field and have to call in a specialist to fix my heart problems just like the next guy. When I ignore the "squealing," it gets me into bigger trouble too. It takes maintenance, people. So let's keep up our regularly scheduled appointments with God, and let's not forget He is the Master and can take care of us better than anything or anyone else can!

Until next time, Lord willing,

Sheri

AND TO VIRTUE, ADD KNOWLEDGE

"Whereby are given unto us exceeding great and precious promises: that by these ye might be partakers of the divine nature, having escaped the corruption that is in the world through lust. And beside this, giving all diligence, add to your faith virtue; and to virtue knowledge" (2 Peter 1:4–5).

Finishing up 2 Peter today, I read some quotes written in the margins of my Bible, which carried me back to a time of spiritual growth in the Lord. Some people don't like to write in their Bibles, and I respect that, but I need to make notations as I read. Don't do something because I say so, or someone else says not to—grow in Christ and allow Him to guide you into growing more and always, always, match it up to the truth of the scriptures! I am a sinner just like you and so is every TV evangelist out there, along with the greats that you and I have looked up to for so long. I will fail you, but God's Word will *never* fail you.

My suggestions are just that—suggestions. As you study, write down quotes or thoughts in the margins of your Bibles, especially those thoughts that will feed your desire to please the Lord, wanting to know His mind, His character, His everything! So the following comments were written on the same page but in different years. Write the date of that comment if possible. At the end of 2 Peter 1, I read, again, my comments, which strengthened me in the area of prayer and trusting God. I was reminded of steps that I took toward His throne of grace where more knowledge awaited me.

- 6/28/09 "The will of God is that *all will* receive Christ as personal Savior. This reminds me that *all* who call on Jesus could be saved, not just a few like some religions teach. It is settled!"

  > "The Lord is not slack concerning his promise, as some men count slackness; but is longsuffering to us-ward, not willing that any should perish, but that all should come to repentance" (2 Peter 3:9).

- 8/28/13—"Mark and Sheri are in the States. Katie goes off to college this weekend!" I like to write good things in my Bible that keep me praying for those in my family. If you write such positive notes in your Bible, then you can rejoice with me on this one.

- 6/27/10—"Our minds should be stirred up by the Word of God." As we get a hold of this thing called "knowledge," our diligence kicks in, and off we go "stirred up by the Word of God." God will have an opportunity (not that He needs anything!) to use us to help others "know" God.

Ernie Mikell, who keeps our buses running and does so many other jobs around our school and church, stays "stirred up" by the Word of God. Several times a week he comes up to me with a truth that he and his wife, Linda, absorbed from the Word of God that same morning in their family devotions. He not only gets excited by the Word, but he gets me stirred up just listening to him! Now, isn't that better than gossip or finding fault of another?

"Wherefore I will not be negligent to put you always in remembrance of these things, though ye know *them*, and be established in the present truth. Yea, I think it meet, as long as I am in this tabernacle, to stir you up by putting *you* in remembrance" (2 Peter 1:12–13).

It is easy to criticize, gossip and judge others at times and shame on us, me included, for stepping away from the filling of the Holy Spirit when all God wants us to do is glorify Him *by His word,* and yet we justify our tongue as it slaps people down day in and day out! If you are a woman who talks a lot, like me, then let's talk Jesus. Women who talk a lot usually say too much to more people than they will remember and thus become known as gossipers, constantly stirring the pot. Let's be remembered for "stirring" up people for the Lord.

Just recently, my mouth got out of control. I went back to my office and shut it up with God's help, opened the door, and to my surprise there stood a parent of one of our students in the school. "Mrs. Loyd, may I talk to you?" I allowed her a few minutes to vent, trying to get a clear picture of the problem, but the more this dear mom revealed, I began to wonder if she knew what the Bible had already said about the problem. So I placed my hand on my Bible and asked, "What has God shown you already about this situation?" She couldn't answer me and admitted to not reading it "lately" but would like to know what it said.

"Tell me about your relationship with Christ." She began to weep. I was taken by surprise because I knew she had family in another country who were missionaries. I assumed she was born-again.

We should never assume that someone is born-again! She had a "knowledge" of God, but did not know Him. I then opened up my Bible, and she and I read the scriptures that lifted the veil from her eyes to the truth that she needed a personal Savior. I cried, as it was so sweet! What a Savior! Now, Sharon, you tongue-slapping woman, you almost missed a great opportunity to share Jesus Christ because your diligence was good, but your flesh jumped in, which almost kept you from finishing the task for the day. I'm glad I went back to my office, confessed, and came out to do His will, not mine.

Also, one of the most dangerous decisions we can make after leading someone to the truth of salvation through Jesus Christ, is to leave them for the rest of the ride, alone. No! These precious souls need more "knowledge." This mom needs to grow with someone along her side to guide her to more truth so that she can begin to give diligence to adding virtue to her faith and to virtue, knowledge; and to knowledge temperance …

Oh me, help me, Jesus! I am the worst sinner of all, but by God's precious saving grace, I will practice this self-discipline called *temperance*. Will you join me?

Until next time, Lord willing

Sharon

YOU CAN MAKE IT!

This lesson is a great idea for a ladies' Bible study. Assign the "I AMs" to different ladies or have them volunteer and allow them to look up the scriptures and seek out a personal testimony to share with the ladies. When more ladies are involved, excitement grows.

I recently started a study on the words *I AM* in the Bible. I searched for every verse where God declared Himself as an *I AM* and wrote the reference down in my notebook along with what God said He is. My hand began to cramp as I got to the twentieth chapter of Leviticus. My heart was swelling and almost burning in my chest as I took note of what I was reading. I searched for the last instance of this type of declaration, and I found it in Revelation where He declares Himself to be the root and offspring of David, the bright and morning star.

I don't know why we feel the need as women to seek out some "new thing" to reassure us that God is exactly who He says He is. I don't know why we forget from one prayer request to another that God is faithful and just, a provider, and a shield. Why in our darkest nights of trials do we not seek the bright and morning star to help guide our way?

Why do we constantly deny the power of God in our lives? We shouldn't enjoy crying about our problems more than we relax in the knowledge that we have a problem solver observing our every moment. Yet we struggle against our flesh and our desire to have a perfect life instead of allowing the almighty to have His way. We post our request on Facebook or mention it in prayer meeting, but we won't spend more than five minutes alone with God to talk to Him about it or read what His Word already says about it. You know it's true, so don't get mad at me. I am just as guilty as the next woman.

You and I have made some headway on this journey to know God better, but before us lies a blind path that can only be crossed by faith, faith in who God has declared Himself to be. He didn't say He *would* be the bright and morning star one day. He said He *is*. That path before us can be and will be illuminated by God as we move forward in trust.

What is it today that is holding you back from releasing it all to God? Do you really think you are the first person to be in whatever situation you are in? It may be the first time for you and you feel broken, alone and without hope, but God has not changed from Eve's day until now, nor will He ever change. He loves us. He loves you. God has a way to get the glory in your life, no matter what your situation is. Are you holding back glory from God? Are you shadowing the Almighty's presence by your despair? Are you humble enough to admit that you have not been trusting Him?

Look, the hurts you feel today are real, and you need to understand that you are not worthless. God wants to validate your life by producing joy in your spirit again. Did you know that when you woke up this morning, He already was aware of the weight on your shoulders, but He is also standing right beside you, waiting for you to allow Him to bear the load? He is pointing out a path in your life that must be followed, and He is telling you that it will be tough at some points, but to remember that He is:

Your Shield
Your Rock
Your Protector
Your Guide
Your Light
Your Joy
Your Strength
Your Peace
Your Help
Your Salvation
Your Listener
Your Friend
Your Judge
Your Forgiver
Your Saviour
Your Healer
Your Refuge
Your Song
Your Tear Catcher
Your Teacher
Your Everything

He is the Lord *your God* and He wants you to rely on *Him* for the answers you need today. He wants to fill your mouth with the words to speak to your enemy. He wants to fill your heart with forgiveness. He wants to fill your mind with good thoughts. He wants to hear your prayers. He desires to walk with you as you do His will. That is just how much you mean to Him. Can you let go, or *will* you let go and allow Him to do His part?

You may feel like lashing out at me and screaming about how your life is in shambles. I understand; I have been there. It isn't fun, no one likes it, and you wish it would just all end. I get it.

You don't want to deal with the lot that has been cast for you. I know. But you don't have to go through it alone. There is a perfect way in front of you. You can't see it, but the Light is already there, because He inhabits eternity (Isaiah 57:15). He is before you, behind you, and beside you.

You can make it. If you fall down today, get back up tomorrow. God will still be God, and He will still answer your prayers.

Until next time, Lord willing,

Sheri

TEMPERANCE, BUT I DON'T WANT TO!

"Grace and peace be multiplied unto you through the Knowledge of God, and of Jesus our Lord." (2 Peter 1:2) I need His Grace and Peace multiplied unto me, don't you?

"And to knowledge temperance; and to temperance patience; and to patience godliness" (2 Peter 1:6).

"But the fruit of the Spirit is love, joy, peace, longsuffering, gentleness, goodness, faith, Meekness, temperance: against such there is no law" (Galatians 5:22–23).

Grandma Baxley was probably the greatest Christian woman I knew before I left Clay County as a teenage girl. She was quite unique if I must say so, and oftentimes as I literally watched her silently wait on others with a smile, I thought she was a type of superwoman! Grandma never drove a car and never left Florida. I don't know if she graduated from high school or not, but this one thing I do know— Grandma knew my God! I used to be critical of her always giving in to help people who just took advantage of her. Her dining tables, three of which she kept prepared, were large and were the main pieces of furniture in the dining room and on the screened-in back porch. Grandma kept a supply of foods for the hungry, and before they left, she sent them away with something to take with them like a jar of her canned black-eyed peas from the shed filled with rows of stored vegetables. Sometimes she would slip out to the smokehouse and grab a slab of pork, wrap it in brown paper, hide it under her apron so Grandpa wouldn't scold her, and slip it to someone. Sometimes, that family would be one of her own children or grandchildren. We *all* benefited from Grandma's treasures of giving! The most unselfish woman in Clay County, Grandma was temperate in all things. From my best recollections of her, it started when she was very young. She kept herself from certain indulgences, and because of that early decision, I benefited along with countless others as well.

God holds His hand out to us with the choicest of His best, and yet because of our weaknesses, we may turn our heels to less of His best. Make sense? This attribute called *temperance* is a mystery to some degree. Just how far should we stretch our minds in order for us to understand that it takes time, a long time maybe, to get rooted in God's Word. And yet, we may still fall flat on our face to get up again! Well, join this family of saved sinners!

We all mess up—wouldn't you agree? Sheri and I have tried our best to help you see that we are real and *not* perfect! If I could crawl into the minds of parents, I would say loudly, "Keep your child in the Word. Practice the Word and don't allow for them when it is in your power to do so, the temptations that would 'govern their passions and affections' in opposition to a holy and righteous life. You will have to be the judge of this and God will guide you! Some things I grasped along life's way as a Christian teen, but some things I did not. Of course with life, we learn, but why not produce some more Daniels! It is possible! We give our children way too much leniency in the area of choice in making decisions that could be detrimental to their walk with God, to really know Him and His Word. Remember: there is always a rattlesnake in a corner *somewhere* to strike our precious children. Don't put them close to the bite!

My Bible (The Open Bible, Expanded Edition, King James Version; Thomas Nelson Publishers, Nashville) defines temperance as "self-control." Self-control over what? I'll let you answer that. At this writing, I'm on *another* eating plan. You know why? I am an idiot and a sugar addict! Who is to blame? Me! I am to blame, of course. I have control over everything that goes into my mouth. I can hardly write about sweet foods without running to *somewhere* and grabbing something to eat. We have to eat, wouldn't you agree? It is my problem, and now I am trying to get it under God's control and not my own. It has been fun, this new way of eating, but let's face it: all diets can be fun for a while. Then ole slew foot comes around. Temperance for me right now is doing what I don't want to do, to do what I should do so I can enjoy the things that are good for me—like making it to my next birthday!

You know in your heart if your weakness is gluttony, intoxicating drinks, exciting passions which could be a multitude of things, temper, and any other indulgence(s) contrary to God's way of life. No way around this one, folks. We are all guilty, maybe some less than others. Good for you if you are on the right road, hands on the steering wheel, looking straight ahead with eyes focused! God bless you! Then help someone else. That is what my grandma did. If she ever had a temperance problem, I don't know what it was. Her stomach was pudgy and jiggled when she laughed, but back then, I thought she did it on purpose for us grand youngins.

The fact remains that if we are truly hungry with a desire to know this Jesus, our God, Creator of all, then we have to admit our lack of self-control in the areas that dominate our minds and our bodies. Hand it over to Him relinquishing our way for the *perfect* way, and then we can move on in our lives. Don't stay in the middle of the road on this one. Trust me; this is the one area most women struggle! It is time to move on.

> "For if these things be in you, and abound, they make *you that ye shall* neither *be* barren nor unfruitful in the knowledge of our Lord Jesus Christ" (2 Peter 1:8).

Isn't that what this journey is all about—getting to know Him? If you need prayer, contact us, privately, and we *will* pray!

Until next time, Lord willing,

Sharon

THERE IS ROOM
FOR EVERYONE

"For we dare not make ourselves of the number, or compare ourselves with some that commend themselves: but they measuring themselves by themselves, and comparing themselves among themselves, are not wise" (2 Corinthians 10:12).

I have two dogs, Valentine and Victoria. Valentine is a German shepherd that appeared here on Valentine's Day last year, and Victoria is my six-month-old Saint Bernard I received as a gift for Christmas. Every morning they come and talk to me and wait for me to pet and scratch them. They aren't like my cat, Nellie, who just wants to be fed and left alone. No, Valentine and Victoria want attention, and they whine and wag their tails and vie for the closest spot to me. They are jealous of each other and bite and push each other out of the way so they can get to me. It is comical, but so much like the way we treat others in our attempt to get at God.

I have spent my life observing Christians being rude and manipulative in order to gain favor with God *and* man. I've done it myself, and I was wrong. I have watched good, God-fearing people leave the ministry because they didn't meet up to someone else's expectations. I have seen teenage girls be turned away from a preaching service because they had skirts on that weren't long enough. I have seen women going through divorce and heartache, rejected because they made a mistake that cost them their marriage. I have seen men lifted up and praised in a godlike fashion only to have lives destroyed when they were found to be just human after all. I have been pushed out of the way, and I have pushed others out of the way for a "spot." It is all very ridiculous and downright shameful behavior of us all. The world sits back and laughs and mocks us and the God we claim to serve as they fill hell and cause it to enlarge itself in order to contain its multitudes. And you and I will be held responsible one of these days.

> "But I keep under my body, and bring *it* into subjection: lest that by any means, when I have preached to others, I myself should be a castaway" (1 Corinthians 9:27).

As we seek to know God and trust Him with our very lives, let us be careful not to deny another sister or brother the same right. God doesn't. He doesn't see skin color, bank accounts, or status. He sees those souls covered with the righteousness of His Son and welcomes all at His feet. Should we be any different?

I love both my dogs the same, I have enough love for the two of them, but I will swat the fire out of the first one that bites the other one. I will make them go lie down until they calm down. I don't want God to make me go "lie down." I don't want to be constantly vying for my position, because it is an oxymoron—my position is secure. I am His daughter, He Loves me, and that is that.

As a missionary, it is difficult to not watch other missionaries and compare, especially when we live in this day and age of social media. I love it—don't get me wrong—but seeing another church bloom and blossom will make you start questioning why your work is so laborious. And if you aren't careful, you will begin jockeying for position instead of contentment.

God has us in the palm of His hands where He wants us if we are submitted and doing His will. He loves the Pastor with thousands of members, and He loves the Pastor with a handful on the membership roll. There is no need for one to step on the other or one to feel less than the other. God loves the woman with the houseful of children, and He loves the woman who buried her only child or knows the emptiness of the barren womb. He loves the college graduate and the dropout. He loves the beautiful and the plain. He is the leader of the brokenhearted and the joyful, the loud and the timid. If we are saved, we are His children.

> "And be ye kind one to another, tenderhearted, forgiving one another, even as God for Christ's sake hath forgiven you" (Ephesians 4:32).

> "But I say unto you, That every idle word that men shall speak, they shall give account thereof in the day of judgment" (Matthew 12:36).

Are you being kind to your brothers and sisters in Christ? Have you looked down your nose at one recently? Have you made a snide comment to your friend behind someone's back? God is watching you, He heard what you said in your office behind closed doors, and He doesn't like it. He won't hold you blameless either. What if you could be the difference today in someone's life who you think is just being hard to get along with but their heart is breaking? Instead of setting yourself up on a pedestal and pushing them out of the way with your words, what if you went and put your arm around them or wrote them a note of kindness? You both could be loved on by God today and not sent to the corner to learn to behave. You just may be the one to help someone else today *stay* on our journey. The car is big enough for everyone, so let's not leave anyone out.

Until next time, Lord willing,

Sheri

I DON'T HAVE PATIENCE
ENOUGH TO BE PATIENT!

"And to knowledge temperance; and to temperance patience; and to patience godliness" (2 Peter 1:6).

It has taken me days to be able to pull together proper thoughts on this attribute of God. Patience. Ugh! If there was a time in history where we experience people with none, it is now friend. It is now! Who has patience? Are you able to picture someone in your family, church, workplace, or school who exemplifies this attribute of God? I honestly believe that my preacher, Dr. Andy Bloom, is one of the most patient men I know. He would disagree, and maybe his precious wife would too. He puts up with the likes of us—*all* of us from every walk of life. There aren't many people who possess this attribute and when you read the kind of patience 2 Peter describes, good luck if you know someone close to you. I know. I know. We all are patient at times, but I'm talking about this patience of 2 Peter 1.

Children are allowed to pitch fits and stomp out of restaurants, demanding that their parents give them their way. Teachers talk about the impatience of their students, and yet they themselves are impatient with their own children and families. Preachers preach on it, especially the patience of Job, but no one, including me, wants to go through what poor ole Job went through to acquire this thing called *patience*. So how in the world do we ever obtain it? We don't, folks! It comes through the knowledge of Him that hath called us to glory and virtue. I call it *getting into the very soul of God Himself.*

> "Now we exhort you, brethren, warn them that are unruly, comfort the feebleminded, support the weak, be patient toward all *men*" (1 Thessalonians 5:14).

Are you patient toward all men? Do we really practice this command?

> "So that we ourselves glory in you in the churches of God for your patience and faith in all your persecutions and tribulations that ye endure" (2 Thessalonians 1:4).

It takes endurance and time to apply this kind of patience.

Why is it that grandmothers are more patient than moms? Why does God teach us to seek the wisdom of the elderly? Why does a pastor show more patience than his congregation? Trials, tribulations, life, being poor, sick unto death, beaten, heartbroken, talked about, spit on, made fun of with bumps so hard and high you don't know if you are going up or coming down—the process of patience is unbearable without knowing that God is in control of your life regardless of what happens day in and day out. Job practiced it before the day of the championship game, folks. I wonder how long it is taking for some of us to get it.

Over twenty years ago, our Sunday school class, the Challengers, began a ministry to one of the local nursing homes. Each month we have the opportunity to share a potluck dinner, devour it, and then go to a place where the elderly are almost forgotten. I have to admit that it is not my cup of tea. For most, it is the last stop before death's final call, but for us who minister to them, it offers an opportunity to share the gospel with those who may understand. Sometimes, they are born-again, but because of sickness, they may not remember. For the others, we sing and sing some more! Patience.

The food stains, the unmatched socks or no socks, the smiling faces of some, and the sad faces of others all await us as we push these special people down the hall to a room where we try to give them forty-five minutes of *something* worth living for! Patience. We sit, we sing, and we turn pages for them, sometimes allowing them to use their one hand that is not paralyzed by a stroke to turn the page of an oversized song book, watching them pull smiles with twinkles in their eyes as if to say, "I did it! I did it!" Patience. Then they touch your hand, remembering back to the day of a daughter or granddaughter, and your heart wants to help them hold their smile long enough to remember that they can still remember *something* worth living for. I sing louder so they can hear the familiar tune from years back or maybe it was just yesterday. They can't figure it out! Patience. I work at it at least once a month with a people who don't know me.

Job was the dad and took his role seriously as a father. He was perfect and upright, one who feared God and eschewed evil. This means he was a good man and avoided all evil, probably avoided the appearance of evil as well. Satan couldn't touch him without God's permission, and neither can he *you!* God gave Satan a little rope in Job's life to test him, putting him under some pretty heavy stuff. God may be doing the same in your life. It's tough but you are wanting to be patient and not lose hope! Job made it and patience was not only born but grew in Job's life. God watches and knows what will happen next, because God knows everything. He watches you and is your biggest cheerleader. He so desires for you to make it across the finish line of patience. Job was becoming stronger for the next test, and he didn't even know it. Job's wife could have had the same growth, but she reacted to life's trials like most of us have at some point in our lives, becoming a bitter woman. Maybe I would have too. How are *you* doing?

Next, Satan is allowed to touch his body and the world scatters from Job. He stinks; he is nasty and repulsive to look. But not to God! Job didn't allow Satan to win, folks. He could have, but God knew Job had it in him to endure to the final straw at a time when there was nothing else to happen but death! Oh, how happy Job must have been once he endured the heavy monster of a trial and, as a result, was blessed at the end more than he was at the beginning! I can see Job looking back, thinking but thanking God out loud for giving Him the strength to endure such pain and agony. Thank God for Job's example.

I want to be blessed more at the end of my life than at the beginning. How about you? Crawl inside of God's soul and get a firm grasp on this thing called *patience* and know *He knows* how much you can handle. He knows! In the end, *you* win. God has already won the battle anyway whether you choose to allow Him the opportunity to know Him, really know Him!

Patience can begin to grow in you, today.

Until next time, Lord willing,

Sharon

MAKE SENSE OF THE BIBLE

Now Peter and John went up together into the temple at the hour of prayer, *being* the ninth *hour*. And a certain man lame from his mother's womb was carried, whom they laid daily at the gate of the temple which is called Beautiful, to ask alms of them that entered into the temple; Who seeing Peter and John about to go into the temple asked an alms. And Peter, fastening his eyes upon him with John, said, Look on us. And he gave heed unto them, expecting to receive something of them. Then Peter said, Silver and gold have I none; but such as I have give I thee: In the name of Jesus Christ of Nazareth rise up and walk. And he took him by the right hand, and lifted *him* up: and immediately his feet and ancle bones received strength. And he leaping up stood, and walked, and entered with them into the temple, walking, and leaping, and praising God. And all the people saw him walking and praising God: And they knew that it was he which sat for alms at the Beautiful gate of the temple: and they were filled with wonder and amazement at that which had happened unto him. And as the lame man which was healed held Peter and John, all the people ran together unto them in the porch that is called Solomon's, greatly wondering. And when Peter saw *it*, he answered unto the people, Ye men of Israel, why marvel ye at this? or why look ye so earnestly on us, as though by our own power or holiness we had made this man to walk? The God of Abraham, and of Isaac, and of Jacob, the God of our fathers, hath glorified his Son Jesus; whom ye delivered up, and denied him in the presence of Pilate, when he was determined to let *him* go. But ye denied the Holy One and the Just, and desired a murderer to be granted unto you; And killed the Prince of life, whom God hath raised from the dead; whereof we are witnesses. (Acts 3:1–15)

Did you read the above passage? If not, don't read any further until you have, because I am going to teach you a few quick steps to getting more out of your Bible reading time.

One of the prime reasons Mom and I decided to write this book was to encourage women to read this Word of God, thus getting to know the Lord more personally. We have made a case for the reading of the truth, and I hope that you have found tidbits here and there that have encouraged you in your walk with the Lord and your time spent with Him during the day. But don't ever let the Bible become just "commonplace." This Word of God will create a hungering and thirsting for God Himself. We can walk away every morning spiritually satisfied. The only way that this can happen is if you pay attention to what you are reading. Let me explain what I mean.

In Acts 3: 1–15, you will read about the lame man at the gate of the temple, correct? But, what else did you get from it? Here are some questions to ask yourself every time you read the Bible.

1. Who wrote this passage?

2. To whom was it written?

3. When was it written?

These three simple questions will lead you to dig just a little deeper and go a little farther than just crossing off your Bible reading chart and going about your day. It is great to read the Bible, but if you don't understand what you have read, it doesn't do you much good, does it? It would be like going to a buffet and only getting pudding every day. You would walk away feeling full, but in a little bit, you would be starving again. Besides, it isn't healthy, and neither is it spiritually healthy. We need to put some meat and potatoes on our plate, so to speak.

Okay, so here is what I did when I read the above passage. I made myself think on the lame man. In chapter four we find out he is in his forties. That's my age. So, what would it have been like to me to lay there every day at the gate of the Temple and beg, never having taken a step or stood upright or walked around? I wouldn't have enjoyed that very much. Then I thought a little deeper. If this passage took place just weeks after Jesus was crucified, then perhaps this lame man had seen Jesus pass by and knew of the miracles He did and the lame and blind He had already healed. Wonder why his parents had never taken him to see Jesus? Was he cynical about the powers Christ possessed? Or was he just a sullen man who had given up hope of anything good ever happening to him? Then I got to thinking, what did he do the day Jesus was crucified and the earth shook and it was dark outside when the sun should have been shining? Did all of these events cause him to begin questioning if Jesus was indeed the Son of God?

All of the thoughts I had about Acts 3, caused me to go and read the account of the crucifixion in the Gospels. It made me think on the current events of those days. It led me on a trail to read and study. Why? Because I took time to think about what I had read in my regularly scheduled reading. And that is what I want you to learn, also. The Bible will begin to make sense to you as you ask the Holy Spirit to read along with you and guide your thoughts. You will get so much more out of God's Word!

After I studied about the lame man, I thought on Peter and then about faith. Go back and read the passage again and do some thinking. Try and glean as much as possible from your time with the Lord as you can. The Bible is a living Book and there is no end to its depths.

Think about this verse:

> "The counsel of the LORD standeth for ever, the thoughts of his heart to all generations" (Psalm 33:11).

When you read and study, you are getting a glimpse of the thoughts of the heart of God. Enjoy getting to know our God. He wants you to know Him.

Until next time, Lord willing,

Sheri

STICK WITH THE STUFF!

But godliness with contentment is great gain. For we brought nothing into *this* world, *and it is* certain we can carry nothing out. And having food and raiment let us be therewith content. But they that will be rich fall into temptation and a snare, and *into* many foolish and hurtful lusts, which drown men in destruction and perdition. For the love of money is the root of all evil: which while some coveted after, they have erred from the faith, and pierced themselves through with many sorrows. But thou, O man of God, flee these things; and follow after righteousness, godliness, faith, love, patience, meekness. (1 Timothy 6:6–11)

According as his divine power hath given unto us all things that pertain unto life and godliness, through the knowledge of him that hath called us to glory and virtue (2 Peter 1:3).

I looked across my desk at a young man quite handsome and his proud parents as they listened to me advise them of a few necessary steps in this journey called *life after graduation*. This young man had no idea, really, of what he wanted to do. Money for college was no issue, which is not the norm for most of our seniors. Both parents had dreams of a prominent future with a six-digit income for their son. We looked at his career results, and I spurted a few more questions, hoping to whet his appetite somewhat just to get an idea which direction to take.

Of course, the obvious question was, "Son, what has God shown you thus far in your walk with Him?" His parents were not aware that he was considering a Christian college, and I needed to respect his decision to wait and tell them, but something inside of me wanted to scream out, "Hey, can't you see this one decision, right now, is the launching for all other decisions in life?" I held my tongue and applied some patience in the matter until God gave me the green light.

"What do you really *want* to do? I asked.

"Play golf!" he declared while his dad chuckled and I smiled. Mom didn't know what to say.

"Will you be able to support yourself, a wife, and ten children, playing golf?" We all laughed together, but soon thereafter, the boy revealed his plan of sending his application to a Christian college. His parents were shocked. They had no idea. Where in the world had they been all these years? Somewhere in his education with us, he grabbed the fact that he needed to continue his Christian education beyond our academy. I had to make myself contain these words, "Well, bless God. Will somebody shout hallelujah?"

God's plan, what is it? The sooner in life we tackle this question, the sooner we will have more opportunities to reveal the character of our awesome, wonderful God! This sixth attribute, godliness, mentioned in 2 Peter 1, is one that is challenged daily in our society. According to Webster's 1828 dictionary, *godliness* is defined as

> n. from *godly.* Piety; belief in God, and reverence for his character and laws. 1. A religious life; a careful observance

of the laws of God and performance of religious duties, proceeding from love and reverence for the divine character and commands; Christian obedience.

We have an unscriptural view of godliness and I believe it must stem from so much deception in some churches. Preachers have been known to teach that gain is a good sign of living right, sending your money all over the world and other erroneous interpretations of godliness. This is wrong folks, pure erroneous teaching of God's Holy Word. In the Bible, 1 Timothy 6:5 says, "Perverse disputings of men of corrupt minds, and destitute of the truth, supposing that gain is godliness: from such withdraw thyself."

Godliness with contentment is almost unheard of. The scriptures teach in 1 Timothy 6:6 that "godliness with contentment is great gain." Our gain should be things of a spiritual nature. Do you see what I see in today's Christians, especially in women? Too many women are unsettled and dissatisfied. There's constant "switch out" of homes, furniture, vacations, various getaways, clothes, redo this and replace that, and never satisfied!

We've all experienced it to some degree, and there is certainly nothing wrong with a new or improved look to something, but I am seeing more and more young people who cannot get enough of any one thing simply because they practice what they see around them. We have given them too much too soon! My young friend has had to work for nothing! It isn't his fault, and the parents are trying to make it easier for him than they had it. So, Sharon, what does godliness have to do with young people not being able to make up their minds about their future? Glad you asked.

God's Word teaches us that when we have too much of something in the world, we may fall into a kind of temptation that will slowly pull us away from knowing God and His longtime plan for our lives. Haven't you noticed that the decision to read and study God's Word *every day* has made a marked difference in your outlook on life? Sheri and I make grammatical errors, use words that some people have to imagine the meaning of, but one thing we cannot fail in is this fact: to know Him is to spend quality time with Him, and as you spend quality time with Him you will desire to be *like* Him, which is godliness! Godliness cannot happen quickly. It takes time with His precept upon precept, God's Word day in and day out. Therefore, godliness has to be taught in the home, and then it doesn't always pan out the way we dream it should. You know why? Our youngsters have a will all of their own.

Stay with the stuff! Don't move with every wind of doctrine. Our children and our grandchildren need us to be faithful standing firm in God's way, adding godliness to patience or their plans may be to just "play golf." Certainly, playing golf could be fun and relaxing, but God requires much, much more. The detour ahead in their life may cause them to fall off the edge. Be strong; run with the power of the scriptures, reeling them back to safety.

The warning has been given to us in verses 9 and 10 from 1 Timothy 6, "But they that will be rich fall into temptation and a snare, and into many foolish and hurtful lusts, which drown men in destruction and perdition. For the love of money is the root of all evil; which while some coveted after, they have erred from the faith, and pierced themselves through with many sorrows." Godliness is the opposite! Focus on being like God as verse 11 states, "But thou, O man of God, flee these things; and follow after righteousness, godliness, faith, love, patience, meekness."

Until next time, Lord willing,

Sharon

GOT A DEAD BATTERY?

"It is the spirit that quickeneth; the flesh profiteth nothing: the words that I speak unto you, *they* are spirit, and *they* are life" (John 6:63).

"But if the Spirit of him that raised up Jesus from the dead dwell in you, he that raised up Christ from the dead shall also quicken your mortal bodies by his Spirit that dwelleth in you" (Romans 8:11).

"For as in Adam all die, even so in Christ shall all be made alive" (1 Corinthians 15:22).

"Great *are* thy tender mercies, O LORD: quicken me according to thy judgments" (Psalm 119:156).

"*Thou*, which hast shewed me great and sore troubles, shalt quicken me again, and shalt bring me up again from the depths of the earth" (Psalm 71:20).

This past week Amelia, my youngest daughter, did her schoolwork at night so the next day she and I could go into town and run errands. We love these times when we can get out together and have a girls' day, so we hurried through breakfast and morning chores. I gave my round of kisses and goodbyes to the boys and jumped in the car, very pleased with myself that we were getting out so early. As I turned over the ignition in the car, my spirits fell from soaring heights to drowning in the depths of the sea as I heard that infamous click of a dead battery. I don't know why I even bothered to try it again, but I did and sadly was met with the same result. Amelia and I got out of the car and Mark came out to see what he could do. A man who works on the farm came over and jumpstarted us, but Mark was afraid for us to go into town by ourselves, so we waited while he finished up his work and got dressed.

Several hours later, we were on our way, but plans were now changed because so much time had been wasted by trying to revive the dead battery. I rearranged the order in which we would run our errands while Mark was at the mechanic with the car. We were already struggling financially because of the dire need for new tires and an unforeseen bill that took all our emergency cash, so having to buy a new battery didn't help our situation. But I decided God must have known about it, and I wouldn't get discouraged. We decided to stop at the post office and check our mail really quick, and boy, am I glad we did. I had a letter from a dear couple in the States who had sent us their yearly support. I pulled out my phone, thanking the LORD for technology, and went to my bank app and deposited the check in just a few minutes. Here we were wondering how we could stretch our dollars, but God had already provided, several weeks before that day!

Do you ever just run out of steam? I'm not talking about being tired after a long day's work, but have you ever been completely spiritually spent? Do you ever feel like you don't have anything left to offer? In the ministry, it is easy to get tapped out if you have several counseling sessions with people who are needing a boost from the Word and they come to you for it. Sometimes as you listen, you are thinking to yourself, "Lady, if you only knew how much I wish I could get a jumpstart today too!" Am I right? So, after some careful thought and analyzing I want to share with you what God can do for you on the days when you spiritually have a dead battery:

1. *Read* God's Word.

> "It is the spirit that quickeneth; the flesh profiteth nothing: the words that I speak unto you, *they* are spirit, and *they* are life" (John 6:63).

Read *His* Word until you hear from Him. Yes, it may cut into your Facebook time, it may cause you to miss your morning jog or third cup of coffee, but it is the difference between a day of spiritual failure and success.

Jesus told His disciples that it is the Spirit that quickeneth ("makes *alive*") and the words He spoke had life. We *need* that life. We need it every single day.

2. *Avoid* anything that continuously drains you.

What do I mean by that? Well, every one of us has pet sins that hound us day in and day out. For some, it is anxiousness, worrying, and fretting. For some, it is rash behavior, quick on the draw with our tongues and actions. For others, it may be useless conversations that we already know the answer, but we continue to talk and talk and talk! For some it is being alone too much which may result in isolation and depressive behavior. You alone can determine what it is in your life that is sucking the life right out of you.

> "Perverse disputings of men of corrupt minds, and destitute of the truth, supposing that gain

is godliness: from such withdraw thyself" (1 Timothy 6:5).

Sometimes we need to not pick up the phone, not respond to a message or check the e-mail. If we are running low on spiritual energy, we need to just stay as close as possible to the power source of God's Word and the preaching of that Word.

> "Quicken me, O LORD, for thy name's sake: for thy righteousness' sake bring my soul out of trouble" (Psalm 143:11).

3. *Shut down* and *reboot.*

> "For if ye live after the flesh, ye shall die: but if ye through the Spirit do mortify the deeds of the body, ye shall live" (Romans 8:13).

You and I need to mortify (kill) our flesh every morning. It is the biggest drainer of all. We have to die to ourselves. We have to die to our fleshly desires. Does that mean we can't have lunch with a friend? *No!* I am talking about literally and honestly looking at your thoughts and desires and how they are determining your day. We have to decide whether or not we are going to obey Colossians 3:8–10: "But now ye also put off all these; anger, wrath, malice, blasphemy, filthy communication out of your mouth. Lie not one to another, seeing that ye have put off the old man with his deeds; And have put on the new *man,* which is renewed in knowledge after the image of him that created him."

That is the shutting down of the flesh and rebooting in the Spirit!

This could be a brand new week for you, friend. The journey continues. Take inventory of your life. Is there something draining you that you can unplug from somehow? I know I need to care for a few areas myself. Let me encourage you to constantly seek God for that renewing and refreshing of your spirit.

And, if you are like us and let your battery run down to the dead click, God has not abandoned you. He was watching you run around and satisfy your flesh, but He has made provision in His goodness and mercy. He will give you the jumpstart you need in order to get where you need to be. Don't give up and quit.

> "Now the God of hope fill you with all joy and peace in believing, that ye may abound in hope, through the power of the Holy Ghost" (Romans 15:13).

See? There is always, always, always, hope.

Until next time, Lord willing!

Sheri

BROTHERLY KINDNESS

"And to godliness brotherly kindness; and to brotherly kindness charity" (2 Peter 1:7).

"Let brotherly love continue. Be not forgetful to entertain strangers: for thereby some have entertained angels unawares. Remember them that are in bonds, as bound with them; *and* them which suffer adversity, as being yourselves also in the body" (Hebrews 13:1–3).

Webster's Ninth New Collegiate Dictionary definition of *kindness*

n. from kind, the adjective. 1. Good will; benevolence; that temper or disposition which delights in contributing to the happiness of others, which is exercised cheerfully in gratifying their wishes, supplying their wants or alleviating their distresses; benignity of nature. Kindness ever accompanies love.

Brotherly kindness is not seen so much in just the everyday, ho-hum Christian life. It takes a determined effort on our part, not because we don't want to be kind but because we get caught up in our circle of events and could possibly ignore the many opportunities to exhibit this great attribute of our Savior. Every now and then I see the marks of true kindness coming up through our grade school children. Usually it is the child who has been made fun of, ridiculed or bullied because of some physical flaw or disability. I hate to see children made fun of and if I get wind of it, I'm in a dead run to stop it! Children will become quiet, isolate themselves from others, avoid crowds, not eat and many times apply self-punishment to their bodies to somehow, some way divert the real pain caused by an unkind person. God help us! If one of us will do something quickly, we may keep a child from growing up as a rebellious teen to a bitter adult, all because of unkindness.

Jesus taught us to love our neighbor even to pray for our enemies, especially those which despitefully use us. He makes it clear how a Christian should treat others. God's love in us is perfected; it is complete and all we need. It will get the job done, whether in the church with fellow believers or in the world as we come in contact with people who are not born-again. Just by our kind acts, the heart may soften causing the ear to bend toward receiving the Gospel.

My Uncle George didn't get saved until later in his adult life. He was always pulling pranks on people especially family members. He loved a good tease and often was chased off the property by Grandma's switches. He just couldn't keep the strict boundaries she placed upon her children and grandchildren which resulted in many scoldings while the rest of us laughed uncontrollably at Grandma's failing efforts to be firm and mean. I loved Uncle George and cherished my Grandmother. They were a blast!

Grandpa sat on the front porch tapping his tobacco on the tiny paper, ready to roll it into one of his cigarettes. I never smoked, but it was such an art to me as I remained mesmerized by the perfectness of the homemade killer. Most men smoked back in the 40's and 50's; therefore, all of my Daddy's brothers smoked and/

or chewed tobacco. I never thought too much about it until I got saved. We had two spittoons in our church, but when Brother Joe May came to town, he preached against the evils of tobacco. My Uncle George was diagnosed with cancer of the mouth caused by too much tobacco for too long, and was recommended for surgery to remove as much as possible. The cancer was so bad that the doctors detached his tongue, completely, and decided he wouldn't live for more than a few days. Rather than leaving the tongue out, they slapped it back in his mouth and quickly stitched it enough to lie motionless until Uncle George's death...they thought! Uncle George DID NOT DIE. He lived many years after that careless surgery. His speech was terrible not only from a botched up oversized tongue but his left jaw bone was completely removed. With a portion of his face sunken in, he resembled someone with a bad stroke. I helped my favorite Uncle, taking care of him as much as time allowed. He was the kindest man on earth! As a teen age girl I felt privileged to wipe the drool from his mouth, help him out of bed, and get him to the dining room table for a meal which we had to hand feed him for a period of time. My Dad made sure that Uncle George kept an income by having him move into our home doing odd jobs. His strength gradually came back and he was off once more as the Uncle who made everyone laugh but this time, his appearance was different. I can still see his crooked face, bright dancing eyes and hairy body. Uncle George had so much colored hair on his body that it actually came through his clothes! I lie not! He looked like an orange monkey at times. We all loved him dearly.

Brotherly kindness is a difficult trait but very much needed in our lives if we are going to be productive in this life of knowing God and being like Him. The unlovely need our brotherly kindness. Uncle George became a different man having survived such a horrible surgery, but he reached out to the unpleasant people of our small town. He would tell everyone about Jesus, His love for them, and spend hours with people that most of us would never visit. I found myself in the middle of his captive audiences, listening to his embellished stories of a time past. Brotherly Kindness.

Uncle George used every faculty he had to retell the parables of Jesus. He brought us to the feet of Christ on the Mount of Olives. We stood on the shore of the sea while Jesus called to the disciples. Uncle George became the Mary washing Jesus's feet. He became Peter denying Christ and would imitate the sorrow that followed Peter that dreadful night. Uncle George stretched his pitiful tiny arms out to help us capture the moment of the crucifixion of our Savior. We watched, we heard, we understood all because of the intense kindness of a man who was repulsive to look at in man's eyes, but beautiful in our eyes and in the eyes of our God. The helpless, poor folks welcomed a story from Uncle George. He never made anyone feel that they were less than anyone else. They didn't mind his peculiar appearance and would push to get close to him to hear his every word. Brotherly kindness.

Until next time, Lord willing,

Sharon

QUIT CRYING ABOUT IT!

"And the LORD said unto Moses, Wherefore criest thou unto me? speak unto the children of Israel, that they go forward" (Exodus 14:15).

I can't tell you how many times I heard my mama and daddy tell me to "quit crying about it and just do it!" I used to hate walking through the cow pasture at night to go to Grandma's house or to leave Grandma's and come back home. I was scared to death something would grab me. Often, Mama would give me something to take to Grandma's house, and that cold fear would seize hold of me. The boogeyman was as real to me as real can be! Mama would get stern with me and tell me to quit crying and obey.

As I got older, I became more afraid as the tasks became more difficult. Mom and Dad still had the same advice. I remember Dad sitting down with me a few years back when I was in a particularly hard spot, and he simply quoted the scripture. He asked me what I was going to do about it. Basically, he was telling me to quit crying about it and do what was right.

In Exodus 14, Moses had led the children of Israel out of Egypt. He has just done something he thought himself incapable of doing. He was not a superhuman being. Matter of fact, we are given insight in the Bible of how Moses didn't feel worthy of the calling God had on his life. Now here this normal man stands in front of all the people of Israel, who are howling and complaining because Pharaoh's army is marching toward them. Moses tries to rally them by telling them that the Lord will fight for them, and yet in the very next verse, we hear the Lord ask, "Moses, why are you still crying to me about this?" In his heart, Moses must have been silently praying for God to *do something!* Yet God didn't want to hear anymore from Moses; He wanted Moses to *act* and tell the people to go forward.

There are a lot of times when we wrap ourselves in a little security blanket of prayer and chide anyone who tells us to do anything differently. We respond to their counsel with a haughty "I'm still praying about it!" When all we are doing is waiting in fear of what God really wants us to do. The Holy Spirit nudges us and nudges us, and we push it off, blaming our emotions and telling ourselves to just keep praying about the situation.

But maybe God is telling you to stop crying to Him about it and do what He wants. God already knew He was going to open that sea and lead His children to safety and God wanted Moses to get on with it. So, let me ask you, is there something you need to get going on?

Is there someone you need to just walk up to and hug while asking them to forgive you? You are afraid they will tell you off, right? The devil has built all this fear up in us, when in reality, God has told us what to do in Ephesians 4:32 (be kind and forgive). So, there shouldn't be fear in obedience! I wonder how many marriages could be saved right now if someone would just give in and apologize? Forgiveness is not a sign of weakness; it is a sign of someone whose heart is right with God.

Is there something you know God has told you to do? You keep asking Him for His help, but He has already empowered you through His Spirit and His Word, so get up and get going! Don't let fear hold you back when God is telling you to go forward!

Peter was on the mountain and saw Jesus pull back His temporal body and show His true power. Imagine witnessing that moment! You would think after seeing Christ for *who* He really was would be enough to make you never stray again! Yet not long afterward, Peter got afraid and denied Christ three times. He backslid. Don't we all? But just a few weeks later, Peter preached Pentecost, and thousands were turned to God. This a perfect example of someone overcoming his or her fear and moving forward in God's perfect will.

You may have just messed up yesterday, but that shouldn't keep you from accepting God's forgiveness *today* and moving forward! He has a plan for your life. He wants you to keep walking with Him every day. He wants to teach you about these things Mom has been sharing with us from 2 Peter! Hello! Do you see who God used to write that book? *Peter!*

Take a deep breath, confess to God your lack of willingness to act on His commands, and then get up and do whatever it is you know you are supposed to do. Don't lag behind like Lot's wife and turn around and chicken out! You can do it! You may tremble while you obey, but you'll find there is *someone* with a whole lot of strength, bearing you up on His wings! The Lord *will* fight for you!

Until next time, Lord willing,

Sheri

FERVENT CHARITY

"Let every one of us please *his* neighbour for *his* good to edification. For even Christ pleased not himself; but, as it is written, The reproaches of them that reproached thee fell on me" (Romans 15:2–3).

"And above all things have fervent charity among yourselves: for charity shall cover the multitude of sins. Use hospitality one to another without grudging" (1 Peter 4:8–9).

"Charity suffereth long, *and* is kind; charity envieth not; charity vaunteth not itself, is not puffed up" (1 Corinthians 13:4).

"And to godliness brotherly kindness; and to brotherly kindness charity. For if these things be in you, and abound, they make *you that ye shall* neither *be* barren nor unfruitful in the knowledge of our Lord Jesus Christ" (2 Peter 1:7–8).

I have enjoyed studying 2 Peter 1, especially the seven spiritual traits emphasized in verses 4–8. Peter teaches us that God's actual divine nature can be ours simply by taking heed to these precious promises. We can have fellowship with God, partaking in His divine nature. Did you get that? Our sinful selves can sit down with the Creator of *all* and enjoy His company!

I have tried to share with you my thoughts, and I have given examples of real people in my own life for whom I am thankful unto God! We all have these witnesses. Just look about you. Don't avoid them but embrace them. Remember them and tell your children and your grandchildren. Keep them alive!

Isn't it wonderful how God brings it all down where the rubber meets the road? Verse 8 of 2 Peter 1 states, "For if these things be in you and abound"—*or live* (some of you may need to be resurrected!)—"they *make* you that ye shall neither be barren nor unfruitful in the knowledge." There it is again, that word *knowledge* "of our *Lord Jesus Christ.*"

The book of 2 Peter 1:9 states, "*But* he that lacketh these things is blind." Have you ever experienced anyone saying to you, "I just don't see it that way?" That person cannot see "afar off" because he or she is shortsighted. Everything is only as it appears right in front of that person. There is no vision ahead, because the One who gives us the vision to focus upon is not active—alive, if you please—in their lives. They have forgotten. That means it was once there to remember? Um! Where did it go? What did they forget? They were purged, eradicated, pardoned of their old sins! Makes me want to shout, friend! Bless God, we have been forgiven and offered the very nature of our living God *through* Jesus Christ!

Charity is love and the fulfilling of the law. "Love worketh no ill to his neighbour: therefore love *is* the fulfilling of the law" (Romans 13:10).

Uncle George became a walking Bible, but he struggled with his disability as the arthritis began to take over elbow and knee joints. One operation after another kept him close to home. Not only was his face crooked, but now his body was becoming twisted as well. This debilitating disease was not enough, though, to shut my uncle's mouth and wallowing tongue. He would roll his tongue back and forth forming the words the best he could and all the while smiling at anyone and everyone who would listen. Every now and then, he would slip in a tease or two to make us all laugh.

While sitting on a park bench in Jacksonville, Florida, Uncle George observed an elderly lady struggle to cross the intersection. He told me she had arthritis worse than he did. Watching her labor to move one step in front of another, he prayed for her to have relief. He was able to relate to her pain, somewhat, and knew his days were numbered, but she looked younger than him and he felt she needed more time to live. His request unto His God was that the Lord would just transfer her arthritis to him, and he would bear it for her.

When he told me this, I couldn't believe it! What love Uncle George had for the sickly, the down and out, the ones who couldn't do for themselves. Oh, such great agape love, *charity!* It wasn't but a few days that we witnessed Uncle George becoming worse and worse as the arthritis literally took over his entire body. I wonder if a loving Father heard my uncle's prayer and offered him the ultimate opportunity to lay down his life for someone he did not even know!

Now, you can judge this story and frankly, folks, I probably would too, if you told me such an account, but it is as he said. My goodness, how selfish we are at times when a small irritation may keep us from the bountiful blessings of being partakers of His divine nature!

"Yea, I think it meet, as long as I am in this tabernacle, to stir you up by putting *you* in remembrance; Knowing that shortly I must put off *this* my tabernacle, even as our Lord Jesus Christ hath shewed me. Moreover I will endeavour that ye may be able after my decease to have these things always in remembrance" (2 Peter 1:13–15).

Please go back and read the scriptures one more time. My words are nothing. His Words are life and death and offer to us great gain in Christ!

Until next time, Lord willing,

Sharon

LOOK UP

"Then sang Moses and the children of Israel this song unto the Lord and spake, saying, I will sing unto the Lord, for he hath triumphed gloriously: the horse and his rider hath he thrown into the sea. The Lord *is* my strength and song, and he is become my salvation: he *is* my God, and I will prepare him an habitation; my father's God, and I will exalt him. The Lord *is* a man of war: the Lord *is* his name" (Exodus 15:1–3).

Sometimes you need to stop everything you are doing, turn off your phone, walk outside, and look up. If it is raining or snowing, go to a window. Your sky may be blue and cloudless, or it may be gray and heavy with a storm, but the One who made them is neither. He is God, your God. Once you look up, speak to Him. Tell Him just how wonderful you think He really is. Even if your heart feels broken, He is nigh to those with a broken and crushed spirit. He is listening.

I read through some of the recorded praises in the Bible to see what others said to God. I thought on Miriam, Moses's sister as she reached for her timbrel and began praising and singing to God. I thought of the psalmist proclaiming that God was his God, even unto death. I read of Mary in Luke 1 with the most precious words recorded, "My soul magnifies the Lord." I imagined the multitudes singing after God saved them from the Egyptians and what their collective voices must have sounded like.

It brought a stirring to my soul, so I went and sat on the front stoop of my house and looked up. I saw a gray sky, but I said, "Hey, God!" I started to praise Him, but do you know what happened? I immediately turned the attention back to myself and thought, "Who am I to be praising God? I am nothing." A tug of war began happening inside my spirit that I really can't explain, but I imagine anyone reading this knows the exact feeling. The feeling of ineptness, unworthiness, and uselessness began cascading down on me like a powerful waterfall, burying my words of praise. Before I knew it I was ready to stand back up and quit praying. So I raised my eyes again, somewhat timidly and smiled toward the heavens. I told God He was wonderful. I began recounting things to Him that He had done in my life. And before long I was lifting my hands and my voice toward *my God*. I was looking up.

The battles are hard. The deep weary trenches of the trials are dark and seemingly lonely places. You can choose to look down and weep at the mud and mire where you kneel, or you can look up and see *who* it is that is protecting you there while you go through these times. Look up, dear friend. Look up!

The children of Israel had been treated horribly in those years in Egypt, but God had just brought them out. God and God alone had done it. Everyone was singing and praising at the right time and in the right place and in the right direction! They shouted their thanks to Him. They were looking up.

What about you? When is the last time you praised Him for just simply being your God? Not just an off the shoulder comment of "praise the Lord," but praising with all your heart? As I sat out on my stoop, I saw my oldest daughter's shoe that the dogs had found, so I thanked God for paying her bill these last four years in college. I thanked Him for sparing her life in the Amazon when she was just a little girl and sick unto death. I saw a Kit Kat wrapper and thought of my friend, Lonella, in West Virginia who sent my children a big box of candy for Christmas, so I thanked God for her and her family who have often been a blessing to me and the children.

Then I looked over toward the garage and thanked God for the car He provided us four years ago because of our unselfish friends in West Virginia. Then I saw a birdhouse that used to hang at my yellowish-painted home up on Redhouse Hill. The church bought this home so Mark and I could have a house to live in, and, friend, I quietly just started bawling.

God has provided over and over and over again for me, so my praises became more fervent. I couldn't have run out of things to thank Him for if I had wanted. The very fact my fingers are moving across the keyboard typing this is proof of His miracle in saving my life in 2001 when the doctors had given up ever finding out what was wrong. And oh, praise the Lord for all the moments here in Brazil when I have felt desperate and alone but sensed His sweet Holy Spirit come up and sit beside me and tell me He was listening. His Word tells me that He hears me. This is my God and your God. Get to know Him today, every day until he comes for you!

I suppose the purpose of this writing is to get you to take time and look up today. Just let your thoughts linger on Him for a bit. If the enemy comes along and tells you that you aren't allowed, you tell him that Jesus crushed his head once, and you are about to crush it again with your praise to the Lord Almighty! Then began praising our God. For He is worthy. Look up!

"To whom then will ye liken me, or shall I be equal? saith the Holy One. Lift up your eyes on high, and behold who hath created these *things*, that bringeth out their host by number: he calleth them all by names by the greatness of his might, for that *he is* strong in power; not one faileth" (Isaiah 40:25–26).

Until next time, Lord willing,

Sheri

ARE YOU SEALED UNTO
LIFE EVERLASTING?

"**M**rs. Loyd, I need you to fax my transcript to Stetson University."

"I've already mailed it, Trevor."

"I know, but they said they haven't gotten it, and all they need right now is the information on the transcript to begin the process. I have sent my application."

"Okay, I'll do that, but remember: your entrance to Stetson requires an official transcript."

"What is the difference? The grades don't change. It has your signature."

"I know, but it must be secured by our seal in order for it to be 'official,' Trevor. Anybody, anywhere can send a fax to anyone they choose, but to be official, it must bear our seal. Understand?"

"Yes, ma'am!"

I smiled and thought, "I love these seniors. I hope I never lead them astray!"

"In whom ye also *trusted*, after that ye heard the word of truth, the gospel of your salvation: in whom also after that ye believed, ye were sealed with that holy Spirit of promise, Which is the earnest of our inheritance until the redemption of the purchased possession, unto the praise of his glory" (Ephesians 1:13–14).

"And grieve not the holy Spirit of God, whereby ye are sealed unto the day of redemption" (Ephesians 4:30).

"Now he which stablisheth us with you in Christ, and hath anointed us, *is* God; Who hath also sealed us, and given the earnest of the Spirit in our hearts" (2 Corinthians1:21–22).

From that conversation with Trevor, I began to think of the school and church seal compared to God's seal, the Holy Spirit. I'm so glad I have God's seal of the Holy Spirit, aren't you? What an opportunity to share God's Word with students. Sometimes, God just drops these occasions in my lap, but I wonder how many opportunities we have in a day's time when God can't depend on us to speak for Him.

Webster's 1828 Dictionary defines *sealed* as "furnished with a seal; fastened with a seal; confirmed; closed."

I like that definition. *Closed!* But before something can be closed, it must be opened. I did a study on the word "door," and if you want a different perspective on such a powerful word, go and read every verse that contains "door" and I believe you will walk away with an uplifted spirit that may drive you from your comfort zone to a territory of unopened doors for others.

Mrs. Carpenter, one of our second-grade teachers, came to me and said that she had a student wanting to come to my office and talk about her salvation. I immediately sent for the seven-year-old and asked this question, "What is going on? Why are you here?"

She very boldly said, "I need Jesus to come into my heart and save me. He will forgive my sins and I can go to heaven."

"The entrance of thy words giveth light; it giveth understanding unto the simple" (Psalm 119:130).

"Behold, I stand at the door, and knock: if any man hear my voice, and open the door, I will come in to him, and will sup with him, and he with me" (Revelation 3:20).

Umm, wonder how she knew so much already. Her teacher had diligently prepared the ground, plowed it under with the seed, and turned the sprinklers on. "Go get the Book," I told her. She walked over and picked up the big black Bible and brought it to the conference table. As we opened the Holy Scriptures, she read each one out loud and began to see exactly what she needed to do. I really didn't have to do that much. The door to her heart had already been knocked on, and she was ready to allow Him entrance. When she read Romans 10:9–13, her eyes lit up, and she smiled at me. The most beautiful words flowed from this precious young girl. The entrance of God's Holy Spirit was simple, easy, and very comforting as she obeyed the call from Him to be born-again.

After giving her more scripture to read, we walked over to the church, up the stairs to our baptistery, and I explained that she needed to obey the scriptures now that she was saved and this meant baptism. I pretended to be Pastor Andy (that's a joke!) and dipped her down into the make-believe water. She understood, completely, and will remember that day forever. It is important to create a visual for children and for that reason we returned to the Bible, and she marked in the Holy Scriptures, Galatians 2:20, writing her name beside the verse and the date 2/20/15, the day of her salvation. In her own Bible in the classroom, she did the same.

Dr. Jesse Bloom told us more than once that many people get saved as they come to the altar simply because they have placed their faith in Jesus Christ. It is so very important, though, for them to follow through reading the scriptures, marking them, and then actually calling on Jesus to forgive them as a sinner and come into their heart. I agree. Praise the Lord for the door offered to them to walk through and for the sealing of God's Holy Spirit once they enter and the door is shut!

May I ask you this question? Has the ground been tilled for you and turned over and over and the seed planted ready to finish the process? Is He still knocking at your heart's door? One day, the door will be shut, not by me, or by others, but by God Himself either to seal you to your destiny of an everlasting kingdom with Him or to an everlasting hell. Once the door is shut, it cannot be opened ever again. Don't wait and take that chance! God loves you and desires that "whosoever" calls on Him shall be saved. Who is this God? He will save all who call on Him, seal the commitment and prepare an eternal home in heaven. Get to know Him.

"For whosoever shall call upon the name of the Lord shall be saved" (Romans 10:13).

Until next time, Lord willing,

Sharon

OUR GOD IS GREAT

"Behold, God *is* great, and we know *him* not, neither can the number of his years be searched out" (Job 36:26).

I am going to join my voice with Job's friend Elihu and say, "God is great." God is excellent, mighty, and perfect.

Sometimes we are made to doubt those clear facts about God. Many things cause us to question, fear, and then deny who God really is. But if we will just stop up our ears to everything that is contrary to the Word of God, we would find ourselves focusing in on what is real truth: God is great.

Maybe you have come under the illusion that *you* are great. You may have natural talents that make you believe in yourself *more* than you believe in God. This could be why you become so depressed when something doesn't go your way during the day. You have removed your focus from an infallible God, to yourself, a fallible human being.

> "For who maketh thee to differ from another? and what hast thou that thou didst not receive? now if thou didst receive it, why dost thou glory, as if thou hadst not received it? Getting to know Him reveals just how great he really is" (1 Corinthians 4:7).

Any strength or talent you may have is given to you from the Lord, our *great* God. We are nothing in ourselves without His help and strength. When we get to know Him better, we find that we are much better as a Christian sister or brother because we take our hands off of our lives and surrender to His perfect will for our lives.

This past week my daughter was asked by a young man from another Bible college if she believed that there is a perfect will of God for her life. She responded affirmatively and was immediately subjected to a barrage of lengthy retorts on why she was wrong. Mark helped her understand why she said yes and what the difference was between perfect and revealed will of God. I thought on it and read what the scripture says. I think that if a Christian is fully submitted to God and His will, then yes, there is a perfect will of God in our lives.

Semantics would cause us to parse this down to "is it God's will for me to make chicken salad today for lunch or spaghetti?" I think that would be silly to make that the basis of my argument. Why? Because my God is great. I believe He is so excellent, that as He orders my steps, He delights and so do I. ("The steps of a *good* man are ordered by the LORD: and he delighteth in his way," Psalm 37:23.) He is delighted by the choices I make in that I make them while being submitted to *His* will and His will can be nothing but perfect. Why? Because He is great.

For me to rely on Sheri would be an awful thing. And yet, knowing this, I find myself doing just that quite often. Why? Because I am *not* great. I have the flesh to contend with, so therefore I need to contend with my flesh the way my *great* God instructs me to. And how is that?

🖋 Make *no room* for the flesh.

> "But put ye on the Lord Jesus Christ, and make not provision for the flesh, to fulfil the lusts thereof" (Romans 13:14).

That means don't set aside a spot for the flesh. It means we shouldn't harbor anything that can only be used by the flesh and is contrary to the Spirit of a perfect and great God. That means purifying your thought life to the extent you will reject any thought about that teacher you don't like, that preacher you can't stand, that annoying person at church, work, or school. You hold those thoughts up against Philippians 4:8, and if they are contrary, then you reject them. I'm not saying it is easy, but it is right. Want to know Him better? Believe His way and make no room for the flesh.

🖋 Submit yourself to God.

> "For if ye live after the flesh, ye shall die: but if ye through the Spirit do mortify the deeds of the body, ye shall live" (Romans 13:14).

> "Submit yourselves therefore to God. Resist the devil, and he will flee from you" (James 4:7).

Every single day we have to look at God, recognize He is *great* and then purposefully mortify our flesh, our desires, our pride, and our talents. If we are saved, we belong to Him, and we ought to want to do His will. Why? Because He is great.

I have lived in South America in more than one village, and everywhere we travel there must be a trillion spiders. They vary in size, but they plague me with their webs. If I clean one corner of the kitchen window today, you can bet your bottom dollar that there will be a replacement tomorrow. This morning I watched a little red spider furiously weaving an intricate web by a wall outlet. That spider was so concerned with the task at hand that he didn't notice my large frame standing there with a flip-flop in my hand, ready to end its little eight-legged life. Immediately upon standing there, I thought, this reckless spider is exactly like us. We can get so busy working away and depending on our own selves that we forget that it all could be taken away and cleaned up in a heartbeat by our great God. We don't stand in awe of Him anymore as a people or even as a nation. We forget that God is really God. He really is able and will complete His perfect will in our lives. He doesn't rely on our abilities at all, because He is great. He is excellent and He is mighty enough to do whatever He needs doing.

You may want to stop and get yourself in check. If you have been flitting around thinking you are "somebody," maybe you need to realize that tomorrow you could be in an accident that could take away your beauty, talent, and abilities. Then what? God will still be great, because He doesn't change. And He could bring your focus back onto Him very quickly!

If we will realize that He is the ultimate of the ultimate and the powerful, great God, then we will submit with ease.

There is no spin on this writing today; it is cold, hard facts. Either we believe our God is great, or we are believing and living the contrary. Choose greatness today. Submit to His Spirit and do great things for our Great God.

"Therefore to him that knoweth to do good, and doeth *it* not, to him it is sin" (James 4:17).

Until next time, Lord willing,

Sheri

HAS GOD SHUT THE DOOR?

"I am the door: by me if any man enter in, he shall be saved, and shall go in and out, and find pasture" (John 10:9).

Daddy held my arm and asked me, "Well, kid, are you ready?"

As nervous as I seemed, I was ready to step from the opening doorway to enter the church's door where Terry, and my wedding party awaited my entrance. I could see the burning candles and the glittering array of colors from the Christmas trees and lights. All my bridesmaids wore deep ruby-red dresses with matching netted, brim hats. They were so pretty as their dancing eyes stared at me clumsily walking down the aisle.

For a brief moment, fear seized me as I was afraid some officer of the law would run before me, slap some handcuffs on Terry, and drag him out of Anthony Baptist Church while I wailed away! The reception couldn't come quickly enough. My dad was so proud of me and really, in my first eighteen years of life, I seldom disappointed him, but I knew that when he found out that the cedar trees placed in the church had been "borrowed" from a tree farm that night before, he would be so upset.

In reality and putting all kidding aside, I had walked through a major door to another life with Terry Jackson Loyd. It seems we are always entering one door after another. It will never end, will it? One day my life with Terry will end. I'm not sure if I will enter heaven first or not, but I do know all those memories seem like yesterday to me. They are precious, even the "borrowed" tree. I am thankful for all the good memories that live on today as we share with our children and grandchildren. What next? Where do we go after these bodies give up and become dust? Praise the Lord for the opened door of heaven ahead, that is, if you are born again. Who is this amazing God? He is an open door to eternity with Him.

> "Verily, verily, I say unto you, He that entereth not by the door into the sheepfold, but climbeth up some other way, the same is a thief and a robber. But he that entereth in by the door is the shepherd of the sheep" (John 10:1–2).

> "Then said Jesus unto them again, Verily, verily, I say unto you, I am the door of the sheep" (John 10:7).

> "I am the door: by me if any man enter in, he shall be saved, and shall go in and out, and find pasture" (John 10:9).

If you are a Christian, a born-again believer, you have the hope of glory. This opened door awaits those who have already taken care of this business of salvation. Sheri and I have worked hard to share with you how to get to know our Savior better today than you did yesterday, but God forbid that we haven't made sure you are His and He is yours! You can learn all about Him and yet miss heaven. The world is full of knowledgeable, bright and educated people who think they are going to heaven, but are not.

Man and religion keep this world stirred up by offering all kinds of doors with attachments to salvation when there is only one way, my friend. Getting to know God better each day gives you and gives me the opportunity to see just what an awesome God we serve! Be careful who and what you read as you try to feed those desires to know Him. When in doubt, always go back to the Book, the Holy Bible. When we start adding to God's Word and His way, we get into trouble. Man has always wanted to "fix" things for the most part and solve the mysteries of the universe. It is our nature to constantly want answers to questions that sometimes we just don't need to ask because it is already answered!

> "Then spake Jesus again unto them, saying, I am the light of the world: he that followeth me shall not walk in darkness, but shall have the light of life" (John 8:12).

> "And ye shall know the truth, and the truth shall make you free" (John 8:32).

Nothing like knowing "truth" and being free from the sin of bondage! Are you tied down by something? You can be free!

> "Jesus saith unto him, I am the way, the truth, and the life: no man cometh unto the Father, but by me" (John 14:6).

Only through Jesus is there freedom in this stinky world. Walk in the newness of life. Jesus will take care of everything else—*everything*. He stands at the door and knock, knock, knocks. Take hold of His Hand and let Him in. It is time to open the door!

Can you remember a time when you confessed that you are indeed a sinner and cannot save yourself from a place called hell? Can you remember asking God through His Son, Jesus Christ to forgive you and to come and live in your heart? After salvation, did you make your decision public? Have you been baptized by immersion? If not, friend, today is the day of your salvation and the rest of your life. Everything from this point on is decided by *your* decision to receive Him or to reject Him. Just as God closed the door to the ark and none of those crying, screaming people could get in, God will do the same when He calls for the trumpet sound!

> "In whom ye also *trusted*, after that ye heard the word of truth, the gospel of your salvation: in whom also after that ye believed, ye were sealed with that holy Spirit of promise" (Ephesians 1:13).

Once the door is opened to Christ, it closes to eternal damnation. We are sealed by the Holy Spirit! Praise the Lord, friend, we can rest in this troubled world. We can work, be happy in Christ, and have fulfilled lives in Him because of *who* He is, not because of some "thing" we have added to Jesus. Jesus alone is all *you* need. Contact Sheri and me if you are now making this decision. God would not have me make this detour on our road trip, had it not been for a purpose, *you*. He loves *you* that much!

Until next time, Lord willing,

Sharon

WHAT DOES GOD SAY ABOUT PROBLEMS?

"But the God of all grace, who hath called us unto his eternal glory by Christ Jesus, after that ye have suffered a while, make you perfect, stablish, strengthen, settle you" (1 Peter 5:10).

One time as a younger wife in the ministry, I sat and poured out my heart to an older, much wiser Christian lady who quoted the above verse to me. When she shared God's promise to me, I clung to it and it became a Rock to me to keep me from straying in my thoughts of despair during times of trouble and problems.

You and I are going to face problems. There is no two ways about it, friends; we just are. So what does God tell us about how to handle them? Is there a blanket answer for all of us? Can we really know what to do in every situation? Let's take a look at the Bible and see.

We can have different types of distresses or problems and there are promises to be claimed for them all. But no matter which type we are dealing with, we must always begin at the same spot: Prayer.

"In my distress (trouble, problems, afflictions), I called upon the LORD, and cried unto my God: he heard my voice out of his temple, and my cry came before him, even into his ears" (Psalm 18:6).

Our prayers made in truth to God will always be heard. Grab hold of that fact and let that be where you begin "dealing" with your troubles. Pray about them, really truly pray.

Let us ask ourselves what kind of problem are we facing:

🖎 Is it a people problem?

> Only you know the answer to this question. Only you can take steps at resolving this situation. If you have prayed about it, then God will show you what to do.

> If you are in the wrong: Here is Jesus's answer on how to handle it.

>> "And when ye stand praying, forgive, if ye have ought against any: that your Father also which is in heaven may forgive you your trespasses" (Mark 11:25).

>> "Confess your faults one to another, and pray one for another, that ye may be healed. The effectual fervent prayer of a righteous man availeth much" (James 5:16).

>> "Moreover if thy brother shall trespass against thee, go and tell him his fault between thee and him alone: if he shall hear thee, thou hast gained thy brother. But if he will not hear thee, then take with thee one or two more, that in the mouth of two or three witnesses every word may be established. And if he shall neglect to hear them, tell it unto the church: but if he neglect to hear the

church, let him be unto thee as an heathen man and a publican. Verily I say unto you, Whatsoever ye shall bind on earth shall be bound in heaven: and whatsoever ye shall loose on earth shall be loosed in heaven. Again I say unto you, That if two of you shall agree on earth as touching any thing that they shall ask, it shall be done for them of my Father which is in heaven. For where two or three are gathered together in my name, there am I in the midst of them" (Matthew 18:15–20).

Much of what we encounter with day-to-day people problems can be solved in an instant by following God's plan of forgiveness. I have seen *huge* people problems resolved by a simple hug and an "I'm sorry."

So my answer to "can God solve my people problems" is, "Yes, He sure can."

But what if we are being manipulated and are totally unaware of another person's plans? Like, let's say, Uriah in the Bible. The poor man was just doing his job, fighting for King David, and all along he was being betrayed, humiliated, and ultimately killed because of the sinful plotting of another human being. And David wasn't just anyone—he was God's chosen man for the throne! So, what then? Is there a solution? Yes.

"Dearly beloved, avenge not yourselves, but rather give place unto wrath: for it is written, Vengeance is mine; I will repay, saith the Lord" (Romans 12:19).

Give it to God. Let Him deal with it in His *perfection* and His *greatness*. While you wait on Him, claim these verses:

> "Say not thou, I will recompense evil; *but* wait on the LORD, and he shall save thee" (Proverbs 20:22).

> "Recompense to no man evil for evil. Provide things honest in the sight of all men. If it be possible, as much as lieth in you, live peaceably with all men" (Romans 12:17–18).

> "Which is a manifest token of the righteous judgment of God, that ye may be counted worthy of the kingdom of God, for which ye also suffer: Seeing it is a righteous thing with God to recompense tribulation to them that trouble you" (2 Thessalonians 1:5–6).

> "The LORD is nigh unto them that are of a broken heart; and saveth such as be of a contrite spirit. Many are the afflictions of the righteous: but the LORD delivereth him out of them all" (Psalm 34:18–19).

✒ Is it a physical problem?

Maybe it isn't a people problem. Maybe your problems are physical? Is there an answer? Yes.

God may not remove it or heal you from it if His plans are greater than your physical suffering. So, He gives you His promises of how to endure:

"And he said unto me, My grace is sufficient for thee: for my strength is made perfect in weakness. Most gladly therefore will I rather glory in my infirmities, that the power of Christ may rest upon me" (2 Corinthians 12:9).

A preacher friend of ours said that when I can't do something for God's kingdom because of some physical, emotional, or financial weakness, it allows God to manifest *His greatness* by doing it anyway. It allows God to develop in me a reliance upon Him by forcing me to realize I cannot do these things in my own strength.

I suffer daily from arthritis. Not just a little but a lot. People have made fun of me for acting "old." I laugh with them, but inside I am crying. They think I am exaggerating or being funny when in reality it hurts every time I have to stand and walk. It is not easy to deal with pain people cannot see. I hurt almost 100 percent of the time. I have carried a lot physically in my life due to the extremes of where our ministry has taken us in the world. And I literally have paid for it in my body. Sometimes I pray that God would remove it and help me feel better as I try to care correctly for my body. But He hasn't removed this from me. He hasn't delivered me from physical pain. So do I quit trusting in Him? Do I determine that I must not be important to Him? Absolutely not. I trust in His grace. It can be made perfect in me. And one day if Alzheimer's completely takes my memory, I hope that someone will read the Word of God to me and comfort me if I have forgotten that His grace is sufficient. Know Him, friend, and by His precious true Word, get to know Him even more.

🖎 Is it a spiritual problem?

Maybe your problems are not people related or physically related. Maybe they are Spiritual. Is there an answer? Yes.

> "Salvation belongeth unto the LORD: thy blessing is upon thy people. Selah" (Psalm 3:8).

There is *no spiritual* problem that does not have an answer. And the answer lies with the LORD. Period.

> "If we confess our sins, he is faithful and just to forgive us our sins, and to cleanse us from all unrighteousness" (1 John 1:9).

"There is therefore now no condemnation to them which are in Christ Jesus, who walk not after the flesh, but after the Spirit" (Romans 8:1). (You can *not* be condemned for your past if you are walking after the Spirit in the present!)

> "There hath no temptation taken you but such as is common to man: but God is faithful, who will not suffer you to be tempted above that ye are able; but will with the temptation also make a way to escape, that ye may be able to bear it" (1 Corinthians 10:13).

So the spiritual problem has a solution; confession and then faith in God that He will do what He said He would do.

What I am trying to get us to see today is that *in God*, there is a solution. He gave us His Word, and we ought to use it in order to confront any problem we face. And in the end, we will have peace, be stronger, and be settled. Isn't that a wonderful promise? You could just claim that! Ask Him to allow you to experience what it is to be settled. He will do it for you every time. You just have to follow Him and not try and go off in your own direction.

Are you suffering today? Then be kind, because the chances are the lady next to you is suffering as well. Let's help each other instead of making the way more difficult.

Until next time, Lord willing,

Sheri

DO YOU SPEAK
STINKIN' WORDS?

"Let no corrupt communication proceed out of your mouth, but that which is good to the use of edifying, that it may minister grace unto the hearers" (Ephesians 4:29).

If you talk to people long enough, it is pretty easy to find out their belief systems in the matters of heartache, victories, church, family, career, and life in general. It doesn't take long to discover what their relationship is with God either, whether they have trusted His Son as their Savior or just know about Him for one reason or another. It all comes out in conversation, which is our manner of life, according to the scriptures.

Mrs. John R. Rice, wife of the greatest writer on faith that I know, was an unusual woman. She spoke in scriptures. I've never known anyone who walked so closely to God as this dear gracious lady. Mrs. Betty Bloom, Dr. Jesse Bloom's wife, was such a lady as well. To God, people would remember me for a little of what I observed in these spirit-filled women. They both are in heaven now, but their words live on in many, many women.

My tongue is so long it comes out and slaps me almost every day! I hate it, don't you, if you struggle with your words? Marlene Evans, writer and college professor, now resides in heaven, but she taught many of her students and ladies on the sins of women and their tongues. Thank the Lord He gave me enough women in my life to help me know there was hope for me, after all and, there is hope for you. Our tongues can minister grace, or they can corrupt everything and everyone around us. As you draw nearer to knowing God, this one truth will be your peace in times of great distress.

This is a gross illustration but very effective for children as they finally admit to saying inappropriate words or passing one tale (untruth) after another. Just recently a young man and his friend came to my office to let me know that another young lad had called a group of girls a very abominable name. After listening to their version, I had them fill out a "Confession of Someone's Fault."

I immediately went to the classroom of the accused and asked him this question, "Where in the world did you hear such a word as you called these girls?" Without hesitation, he said, "My mama!" I was shocked, truly, to think he blamed his mom, but at the same time, I knew it could be possible as we all make mistakes.

"Do you know what that word means, son?" With tears welling up in his eyes, he answered "Yessim, a female dog?"

Well, I knew at that moment it was time to notify the mom, but before I did, I told him, "When you say words that hurt, it is like spreading a fire that cannot be quenched. The aftereffects are so damaging. Do you understand?"

"Yessim, I do. Mrs. Loyd, I am so sorry. My mama is going to be so mad at me."

I wanted him to see that not only was it a sin for him, but that he caused others to hear and smell his stink, and for that, he would answer to God as well. I know it is a crude illustration, but you *do* get the picture, don't you? You know, we are no different than this child when we "proceed" with corrupt communication.

"That ye put off concerning the former conversation the old man, which is corrupt according to the deceitful lusts" (Ephesians 4:22).

That ole man (woman) is still there and she slips in, on the front lines to make her attack. If you don't watch out, she goes for the kill and the stink begins!

I love cilantro not for the flavor so much, but for the smell as I eat my salad, but if I don't take care of it, it becomes the biggest stink in the bottom of my refrigerator and is good for nothing except for the coyotes and buzzards. They'll eat anything! The rot, odor, and spoil corrupts everything around it. Will you think with me for a moment and take the time to examine the many ways we cause others pain as our corruption multiplies in our homes and in our work place?

Words that kill:

- Can't you do anything right?

- You stupid fool. How many times do I have to tell you?

- I don't know how she puts up with him. I tell you if I was married to him I would—

- Have you seen her new hair color? Oh my word!

- And to think she was raised better than that.

- Well, if they had raised her right, she wouldn't have done—

- I don't know why Pastor harps on—

- What's wrong with —? It's not *that bad!*

- How many times should he forgive her? He needs a life too, don't you know!

- He should just divorce her and get it over with.

If you are kin to Eve, you probably have more to add to the above list and have realized that these ten are a drop in the bucket to what we, as women, have said over and over! Oh me, God help us all. Now take each one and flip it by thinking to do the opposite or by using words that help instead of hinder someone's spirit. Go back to Ephesians 4:29, "Let no corrupt communication proceed out of your mouth, but that which is good to the use of edifying, that it may minister grace unto the hearers." Did you get that? Grace unto the hearers, we have an obligation to proceed with grace for our listeners, folks! Who is our God? Knowing this scripture is one thing but practicing this scripture is another!

Admit it: it takes patience and temperance to stop and then proceed with righteousness.

> "But unto every one of us is given grace according to the measure of the gift of Christ" (Ephesians 4:7).

Jesus Christ has provided for you and for me the grace we need to keep that harmony especially in the church where fellow believers work, pray, sing, and worship together. We have been issued the gifts to do what we cannot do without Christ, but remember as you exercise the gifts He gives, apply His grace. Gifts without God's grace can hurt others. What we say and do may be right but the manner in which we do them, may be harsh and hurtful.

So proceed! Carry on! March in the unity of Christ with a smile on your face today! Are you getting to know Him? I hope so. I am praying that all who read His words find out just who this God really is!

Until next time, Lord willing,

Sharon

Printed in the United States
By Bookmasters